SO-CAJ-497

AS STOLEN ON TV

Stealing the American Dream - One Invention At A Time

This book is dedicated to all the innovators who have been challenged by the patent system, knocked off by copycats or scammed by so-called invention "help" companies, and never give up on the Dream.

Author

Paula Brillson Phillips

Publisher

RANDY COOPER
FOUNDATION

AS STOLEN ON TV

DISCLAIMER:

*The companies and/or individuals referred to throughout this book have been obtained from either first-hand knowledge, stories shared by actual inventors, court dockets, the Federal Trade Commission's or the United States Patent and Trademark office websites and through Internet searches. Other than the stories disclosed, with permission, for the purposes of including in this book, all information about various companies and individuals is already in the public domain and have been lawfully obtained from other sources. The opinions expressed by guest writers do not necessarily reflect the opinions of the author. Legal advice varies based on individual circumstances and this book is **not meant** to provide legal advice specific to an individual's situation. Please perform your own due diligence (or consult with an attorney) to help you determine the best course of action for your particular issue. It is important to note that this book does not personally single out any specific firm, individual or organization for wrong-doing except where such wrongdoing has been gleaned from publicly available documents.*

ACKNOWLEDGMENTS

This book was made possible by all the outspoken inventors who generously shared their stories to support and inspire the next generation of inventors.

Thanks to my awesome kids, Julien and Gaia who encouraged me to share my insights after years of hearing the stories of amazing inventors and their struggles.

Thank you to all the industry players who shared their stories, including: Josh Malone, Lesia Farmer, Tracy Hazzard, Marlene Dumas, Lindsay Carnett and numerous others.

I am especially grateful to Natasha & Fred Ruckel who have spent the last several years going after the bad guys and who not only inspired me to write this book but have played a pivotal role in the book's production.

Many thanks to my mom Carol Toth and Cathy Brillson-Leonard for their feedback and most importantly, their support throughout the writing process.

I am grateful for my business partner, Jessica Sutherland, who, for almost a decade, has shared with me the amazing journey of advocating for inventors.

Proceeds from this book are being donated to the Randy Cooper Foundation (RCF).

****

PUBLISHER: The Randy Cooper Foundation
CONTRIBUTING AUTHORS: Tracy Hazzard, Lesia Farmer, Josh Malone, Fred Ruckel, Natasha Ruckel, Eric P. Rose
EDITORS: Fred Ruckel, Natasha Ruckel
PROOFREADING: William Mentz, Dezso Molnar
ILLUSTRATIONS, PHOTOGRAPHY, BOOK & COVER DESIGN: RuckSackNY

TABLE OF CONTENTS

TABLE OF CONTENTS (CONTINUED...)

AS STOLEN ON TV

INTRODUCTION
FROM RAGS TO RICHES

My mission in life is not merely to survive, but to thrive; and to do so with some passion, some compassion, some humor, and some style. - **Maya Angelou**

People love rags-to-riches stories. I believe it has to do with the human need for hope. If we see an underdog succeed, then it increases our faith and confidence that we, too, can succeed. It makes us feel hopeful that we, too, can change the world, solve a problem, or at least make a decent living with our ideas. Some of the stories contained in the following pages are told by, or are about well-known inventors, or lesser known inventors of well-known products. Some stories have happy endings, while others will simply serve as warnings, as in *don't let this happen to you!*

You may have heard the expression that *if inventing was easy, everyone would be doing it.* We have all heard the stories of many would-be successful entrepreneurs and inventors who are penniless because they enter into contracts that they didn't understand, or enter into partnerships with dishonest individuals. Similarly, we have seen inventors like Joy Mangano (inventor of the *Miracle Mop*®; selling 18,000 mops during her appearance on QVC) who, in spite of adversities (e.g., trusting the wrong partners), emerge as successful entrepreneurs. The purpose of this book is to share with you the trials and tribulations of many inventors whose tales are both cautionary and in many cases, extraordinary, to help you to avoid common pitfalls and heed the warnings of the consequences of certain actions (or inactions) on your journey as an entrepreneur.

I have an affinity toward people who struggle to succeed against all odds, such as spending all their personal savings, working out of their garages, working full-time jobs to support their families while launching their visionary ideas. For various reasons beyond the scope of this book, my journey to becoming a startup lawyer and an inventor's advocate is also a story of personal hardship turned triumphant. As things happen in families - whether from mental illness, addiction, divorce and the like - I became a ward of the court when I was thirteen. With a highly rebellious, 'I know best' attitude, I dropped out of high school in the 9th grade. Many believed I was headed down a path of destruction. Since I got a kick out of proving people wrong, I got a job and hunkered down to study for my GED (high school equivalency exam); working by day to pay my bills and, by night, to teach myself geometry and the like. I passed the GED with flying colors and received my high school diploma at the age of 16.

As a ward of the court, one learns a thing or two from being in the "system." For example, you learn how to be assertive in order to get your needs met. You learn how to escalate matters to higher-level decision-makers and do your research to support your positions, rather than take no for an answer. I learned that by emancipating myself as a minor (meaning that I would be considered an adult even though I wasn't yet 18 years old), I was able to qualify for every possible loan and scholarship to pay for college. That wasn't enough; I wanted to be a pedigreed rebel, and in order to do so, I needed to become a lawyer. Having dropped out of school early meant that I never developed good testing skills; my low score on my law school entrance exam meant that I would have difficulty getting into law school.

However, being hell-bent and determined to become a lawyer, I went to the library (this was prior to the Internet), and through my research, learned I could apply under a special application for minority students – not because of my race, but because I was *economically disadvantaged*. While Harvard turned me down, Rutgers University gladly accepted me! In 1992, I graduated cum laude with a J.D. degree and proudly passed the New York bar exam on my first try.

From the outset, my passion for the law revolved around cases involving big companies taking advantage of little companies, government monopolies stifling competition, and how the law could operate to protect the underdog. I then went out to spend the bulk of my career working with entrepreneurs who were determined to change the world. It's been both rewarding and heart-wrenching; particularly when innovators, who have poured their life savings into an idea, get knocked off or taken advantage of by some unscrupulous partner, lawyer or company, and never see a penny of royalties to show for their blood, sweat, and tears.

If you are tuning in to this message, you are probably a would-be entrepreneur or even a successful inventor who may have encountered difficulties along the way. You may be anxious about the whole notion of disclosing your idea to the wrong people, so you haven't yet taken the plunge into the world of innovating. While every business has its challenges, the business of innovation has been around for a long time, and I'm here to tell you, the mistakes that are made – which can make the difference between *losing your money or making a big profit* – can most often be avoided. Just as parents try to teach their kids lessons to avoid learning the hard way – some kids take the advice, whereas others *do* have to learn the hard way. However, if you have one good idea – just ONE good idea that could revolutionize how we cook/work/sleep, or fill in the blank here . . ., why take a chance that you can blow the *one big opportunity you will ever have* by being a stubborn hard-head who doesn't listen to good advice?

My firm has two types of clients – the ones that bring us their ideas and the ones that bring us their problems. The ones that bring us their problems – such as "someone stole my idea," "my partner cheated me and hijacked my social media campaign," "my product is being knocked off," or "someone failed to pay me my royalties" have – at one time or another said– *I wished I had listened to the advice I was given; I wish I would have read that agreement before I signed it or; I wish I had researched that company before I hired them to help me.*

Of particular concern is when prospective clients contact a law firm after something has already gone awry: They send over their contract and we shake our heads – '**what a dog of a deal**!' - *because it should never have been signed*. They then explain, "But I had my family lawyer/real estate lawyer/Billy Bob, my mechanic review it." "I know I was hasty to sign it, but I really needed this deal!" they exclaim. And then the attorneys get to work poring over the contract trying to get them out of the mess they're in.

The stories of financial, emotional, and personal struggles written about in this book are all real (although, in some instances, names have been changed to protect privacy). The strategies described herein will provide a better understanding of what you need to do to become successful. One of the most important lessons to impart is the knowledge on *how* and *when* to spend the limited resources you have allocated to pursue your idea. Some of the ugly truths that we have witnessed are people who are financially and emotionally ruined in the pursuit of innovation. Whether an inventor was taken advantage of by consultants, invention submission companies, distributors or unscrupulous lawyers (collectively, "The Sharks" of this industry), examples of each are explained in this book. Finally, the bitter truth: Your chances of succeeding with an invention are as close as your chances of winning a lottery. In fact, *only 1 in 5,000 products ever get to the market. These odds demonstrate that 90% of all products never get on store shelves or make any money at all. These odds are meant to rouse, not discourage you. To succeed against these odds, you must believe in yourself and your ideas and take up the challenge.

The purpose of this book is to help you to avoid the pitfalls of inventing. We will impress upon you the importance of doing your homework and having an experienced team to support you. **Examples of early stage questions:**

- *Do you have a great product?*

- *Do you know what the size of your market is?*

- *Do you know the costs involved to manufacture your product and the profit margins?*

- *Do you have some sense of a business model?*

- *Do you have a good team helping you to get it to the market (not just a paid consultant that gets compensated regard-*

less of whether you make any money)?

- *Is your idea protectable? (e.g., patents, trademarks, copyrights)?*

- *Are you comfortable pitching your product?*

- *Have you researched your potential business partner or distributor?*

- *Do you know what a good or bad deal is when it comes to product licensing?*

Some of the stories detailed in this book will make you smile, some will make you cringe, and others will shock you. Absorb them, learn from them, but don't let them scare you away from innovating!

What you will take away is the wisest ways to spend your money when trying to take an idea to retail via a licensing or a distribution deal. It will also help you to avoid many of the challenges that inventors face on a daily basis (e.g., ideas stolen by the very submission companies you send your product to, your products being knocked off and sold on Amazon and eBay, etc.). The majority of the scams in this industry can be avoided (or mitigated) with a little guidance and knowledge. While a plethora of information about inventorship can be found on the Internet for free, we have compiled first-hand experiences from successful (and not-so-successful entrepreneurs) that will not only help you avoid the pitfalls of the industry, but also teach you how to defend yourself, if you've been taken advantage of. The stories you read are real; they impact people's lives on a daily basis, both financially and personally.

TOP TAKEAWAYS

- You need money to make money – inventing is no different. If you are launching a product on a shoe-string, it is likely going to snap unless you follow the three keys as developed by Eric P. Rose (Pages 127-130).

- Before presenting your idea (online or at a trade show) get some protection - file a patent application, register your design, trademark your product name, and/or copyright your images); preferably, all of the above.

- Be wary of TV or Internet ads promising to market your idea for you. Many rip people off for thousands of dollars and never deliver what they promise. In most cases you, the inventor is the best person to market your idea as no one is more enthusiastic than you are!

- Know your strengths and limitations - when you have reached the limit of your expertise, pay a professional.

- Be persistent but not pesky. Confident but not cocky. Passionate but not desperate. Cautious but optimistic.

- Research anyone you consider doing business

with *(you can learn a lot from a simple Google search)*.

- *Hone your pitch and practice with anyone who will listen – buy a table at a flea market or a community fair and try out all approaches to find out what works and what does not.*

- *Most standard agreements are one-sided but they are negotiable – you are an inventor – not a contract attorney; hire someone to negotiate on your behalf.*

- *Get comfortable being uncomfortable – you are always going to be uncomfortable if you are an entrepreneur.*

- *Don't take rejection personally. Your product will either be worth nothing or worth a lot. If it's worth nothing, remain positive, learn from the experience and keep creating.*

- *Create a support network, join an inventors' meetup or a local inventor's association. Share your experiences and learn from the mistakes and successes of others.*

- *Celebrate your successes...large and small. Recognize setbacks for what they are... an unavoidable yet valuable part of the innovation journey.*

1

YOUR BABY IS...
BEAUTIFUL?

Everyone who's ever taken a shower has an idea. It's the person who gets out of the shower, dries off and does something about it who makes a difference. **- Nolan Bushnell**

Most often, new ideas are conceived by working in the kitchen, tinkering in garages, repairing household items, etc. It usually starts with, "Wouldn't it be great if there was some kadoodle that would more easily mop up this mess, stop the dogs from spilling their food all over the floor, keep babies out of cabinets or chop veggies faster," and BAM! An idea is born. The craftier types might even rig up a contraption that solves the problem and they begin using it *all the time*.

Friends or family come over and you proudly say, "Check out my kadoodle," and then after seeing the miracle that is your invention, they say, "That's amazing...I bet you could sell that and make MILLIONS."

The light bulb goes on. You then may embark on an Internet search to see if anything like that exists. You may even contact a company who touts their amazing track record of getting products to market. You may be swayed by their smooth-talking approach to helping you on the path to "sell that and make MILLIONS" and then be persuaded to pay them hundreds, and then later thousands, of dollars for their sage advice.

In truth, many inventors do pay hefty sums to invention submission companies to help them launch their products, but later have little or nothing to show for it - no patent, no distribution deal - just endless invoices and encouragement that they are making great progress on your idea. You've probably seen national TV ads featuring George Foreman who, contrary to popular belief, did not invent the George Foreman Grill, but rather, lent his name to the product as a celebrity endorser (it is rumored that Foreman made over $200M for promoting the grill, whereas John Boehm, the actual inventor, made only pennies on the dollar). You know the pitch: "*Do you have an idea for a new product or invention? How do I get my idea in front of companies? How do I get a patent?*" For answers to these questions, you should call an intellectual property lawyer - not some company who is paying big bucks to a celebrity to promote their services.

Invention promoters (e.g., Inventhelp, Invention Home, Davison Invention, Invention City and many others) advertise services that range from idea review, patent consultation, patent filing and marketing services. Some even claim that they will get you a distribution contract or .... your money back! These companies frequently organize events in fancy hotels and schedule meetings for you to pitch your product or to give you advice.

We attend several invention promotion events per year, and it is consistently the case that only a few products have any market potential. There is no crystal ball but it is easy to see that many products are just a variation of items that are already on the market (how many versions of Tupperware or closet organizers are actually needed after all?!). Other products, upon further inquiry, would be so expensive to manufacture that it doesn't make common sense that the product could be sold to the masses. Still, others are too niched (e.g., how many people would need buy that in order to make this a profitable venture?). We frequently walk away from these inventor forums/trade shows shaking our heads and feeling sad for these inventors because *no one told them their baby was ugly*.

It makes sense, however, that the very companies you approach to help you to launch your invention, or file your patents (and this includes many lawyers who solicit patent preparation through paid advertisements) will get paid from you *whether or not* you ever sell a single unit, so, naturally they are going to blow sunshine up your kadoodle!

You see, inventors, like children, are vulnerable. Their products are like their babies and they have a sense of true emotion and pride in them. They want to be told that their baby is beautiful. It just so happens that, after toiling for hours to perfect an invention, the emotions that often make that belief so heartfelt, so strong, that a particular product will be a huge success, is a primal feeling of hope. Hope, after all, is one of the strongest feelings humans have, powering us to great heights and remarkable lows as we swing like a pendulum between hope and its opposite pole – despair. Hope can also turn us into suckers...

In the 1990s, the Federal Trade Commission (FTC) busted many companies for invention scams, put their owners in jail, and others were sued for millions of dollars. In response, a number of invention submission companies wised up and changed their names and their practices to *appear* to comply with the *American Inventors Protection Act of 1999*.[1] In spite of

1   See: https://www.uspto.gov/sites/default/files/web/offices/com/speeches/s1948gb1.pdf

TIP

As an inventor, you'll be courted by many different companies offering services and silver bullets to turn your invention into a multi-million-dollar seller. Chances are that you'll pay a significant chunk, for a mediocre video and cheap one o'clock a.m. TV ad placements on obscure TV channels. Sadly, these services rarely result in significant sales and can even result in those same companies stealing your product. Don't buy into the hype. This is another way in which 'As Seen on TV' becomes 'As Stolen on TV.'

this law, these invention promoters continue to use the same misrepresentations, inducements and scam marketing practices to collect fees from inventors and yet, deliver no real value in return.

The American Inventors Protection Act of 1999 (AIPA) was enacted to protect inventors by requiring invention promoters to make disclosures to consumers prior to engaging their services.

Title I states: A promoter must disclose to a customer in writing: (1) the total number of inventions evaluated by the promoter for commercial potential in the past five years including the number of positive and of negative evaluations; (2) the total number of customers who have contracted with the promoter in the past five years; (3) the total number of customers known by the promoter to have received a net financial profit as a direct result of the invention promotion services provided; (4) the total number of customers known by the invention promoter to have received license agreements for their inventions as a direct result of such services; and (5) the names and addresses of all previous invention promotion companies with which the promoter or its officers have collectively or individually been affiliated in the previous ten years.

The Act also establishes a Federal cause of action for inventors who have been deceived or misled by an invention promoter. Many clients, however, are deterred from filing a lawsuit as these deceitful companies include a mandatory arbitration clause in their agreements.

To comply with the AIPA requirement, one submission company, namely, Davison openly states in its disclosures that during the past five years, over 280,000 consumers were approached and/or paid them for some type of service – whether it was to develop marketing materials or infomercials or help to identify a licensing agreement. They go on to disclose that, of that total number, approximately 100 people were offered a licensing deal and, of that number, only 15 people made more money than they paid in fees to the invention submission company.

Inventhelp's website discloses that "From 2014-2016, we signed Submission Agreements with 7,039 clients. As a result of our services, 159 clients have received license agreements for their products, and 35 clients have received more money than they paid us for those services." That is a 0.5% success rate; meaning, only a half a percent of their clients ever make any money.

Imagine for a moment you were considering an investment opportunity. If you were told that the odds were 15 out of 280,000 (roughly .01%) that you would make any money at all, would you invest your money? And let's assume for the moment that you are risk averse, and like those odds of .01%, the question is, *how much money would you actually make*? A dollar above what you paid out? You see, the AIPA does not require these invention submission companies (or consultants, for that matter) to reveal the terms of the licensing agreements that are reached or the profits that were reaped. We have seen hundreds of agreements that we wouldn't advise anyone to sign because they are bad deals. In reality, it is not that hard to get a licensing deal when the terms do not favor the inventor. Despite periodic enforcement activities and occasional legislation, the AIPA and the U.S. government do not do enough to protect independent inventors from fraud, misrepresentation, and misleading statements about the success rate of so-called invention help companies.

What is most bothersome is, although these companies are required to openly disclose their poor success rates, they override these statistics by posting multiple videos of success story after success story of how Mary Sue or John Smith got a great deal. One post even shows a satisfied customer posing with a large check and then was told later that she needed to sign an agreement acknowledging that the check was an advance on royalties (and not for *actual* royalties).

The simple fact is: If you're new to product inventing, chances are your baby is ugly. Don't get offended or take it personally, it's all just part of a process. With the right advisors who can provide you with instruction and support, you too can transform your ugly baby into a beautiful one.

Now, of course, we're not talking about real children here - they're all cute.

Lesia Farmer, inventor of the *Trap Door Colander®*, whose product was featured on QVC and sold in big box stores such as Walmart, recently posted a LinkedIn article on "Why inventors are so easily taken advantage of." She aptly states, "We will pay, and we will pay dearly for our babies/children and give them the finest clothes, daycare, nannies, finest education, coolest car, and so on. Inventors treat their product babies much in the same way. They think, 'I want the best for my product' and so, they may be willing to blindly pay an invention submission company. These guys are so well-trained to convince you of just how beautiful your baby is. They will convince you that your baby is unique and has qualities that other babies just don't have! The next thing you know, you are slinging that diaper bag off your arm to get to your checkbook! These guys will call you day after day to remind you of just how awesome your baby is doing and they can't believe how well it is being perceived by the team, etc., etc.! Everyone there is raving about this new baby in the nursery, and you want to hear this; hell, we all want to hear this about our product-baby. But the reality is, not all babies are beautiful." Lesia says her "own son was born with a cone head," and did she think he was the most beautiful thing ever? Absolutely! But, goes on to say with a smile, "The only other people that would have thought so would have been an invention submission company or a paid consultant (LOL).

The other sad truth is that, you may have a great idea that could make millions, but if placed in the wrong hands, your product may never see a store shelf nor will you see a penny of your royalties. Now, here's another rub; should you happen to be fortunate enough to be one of the fifteen inventors whose products are licensed by a third party, the invention submission company actually prohibits you from communicating directly with them at any time. Ask yourself this: Why would a company ever prevent you from communicating with your licensee unless there was something to hide?

On May 16, 2018, World Patent Marketing Inc. and Desa Industries Inc., settled an ongoing investigation and were banned from engaging in the invention promotion business and ordered to pay over $25M in fines. The FTC charged World Patent Marketing with being nothing more than a scam, bilking millions of dollars from inventors. Previous Acting Attorney General, Matthew Whitaker, is currently being investigated for his role in advising this scam company, prior to his appointment.

Today's invention promoters want to send you a free package of information including blank forms and agreements that seem to be of great value (note, again, much of this can be found for free on the Internet). They encourage you to send in your idea for a complimentary review. Wow! They seem pretty legitimate, huh? There are even (fake) reviews and testimonials that support their stellar reputation in the industry. They may even post their "success stories" that showcase a well-known invention, as if they had something to do with its success - but did not. (i.e., Inventhelp had no involvement with the launch or distribution of the George Foreman Grill).

Once you submit your invention to an invention sub-mission company, you will be contacted by phone or email and may hear the following pre-scripted messages:

CONGRATULATIONS! YOUR IDEA HAS BEEN ACCEPTED!

YOUR IDEA HAS TREMENDOUS POTENTIAL!

WE ARE EXCITED ABOUT YOUR PRODUCT!

THERE IS NOTHING LIKE IT ON THE MARKET!

YOU CAN MAKE A LOT OF MONEY!

They may be so bold as to tell you that there may already be interest in your product for a lucrative distribution deal. Now, once you've finished jumping up and down and telling all your friends and neighbors of your good fortune, you will receive another call or email that says, in order to move forward, they must conduct a research report to ensure that your product was actually created by you - it is just customary, they will tell you. The costs for this range from $300 – $1500 for "a research report (depending on the company), but don't worry, if the report shows adverse results (meaning, it can't be done), we will refund your money." Needless to say, we have never seen a negative report - to the contrary - all the reports we have seen (or heard about) indicate that your product has been "cleared" to move forward. But...wait, there's more...most often you will be told that a preliminary patent search will be needed to ensure that your product is unique and novel and not already patented by someone else. This report, which will cost you more hard-earned cash will come back as a standard language (boilerplate) letter called a Preliminary Patent Search. This report is (1) not drafted by a patent lawyer, and (2) completely unreliable. And...big surprise, the letter may also conclude that your idea IS novel, sound, unique and/or practical and useful.

CONGRATULATIONS! YOUR IDEA HAS BEEN ACCEPTED!

YOUR IDEA HAS TREMENDOUS POTENTIAL!

WE ARE EXCITED ABOUT YOUR PRODUCT!

THERE IS NOTHING LIKE IT ON THE MARKET!

YOU CAN MAKE A LOT OF MONEY!

So, you pop that champagne cork once again! You may be envisioning yourself sailing away on that boat you've always wanted, driving a brand new TESLA or paying off your mortgage (as, you've just received your first foreclosure notice in the mail today). Honey, we are on the road to *e-a-s-y s-t-r-e-e-t.*
As you eagerly await news of a promising and lucrative distribution deal, within 10 days to 2 weeks, you'll final-

ly receive correspondence from your "Fairy-Scam-Mother" outlining the next phases of how she is going to help you to achieve your riches (you know, it takes money to make money!). "Someone needs to put together a marketing plan, find a manufacturer, research the costs and suggested retail price, yada yada. But don't worry… you'll receive up to 90% of 'future royalties,' so, you'll recoup that money in no time." I can tell you right now --- 90% of your future royalties will be ZERO because nothing they do is going to get you any closer to a distribution deal. In fact, if your idea is REALLY THAT GOOD, I mean REALLY GOOD, they might pass it along via the backdoor to another company who is then going to take your product - maybe tweak it or rename or just sell it as is and, you'll never see a dime.

Now, before any of these shenanigans begin, unless you shut them down **immediately**, with *clear and concise* language, the next thing that will happen is, you'll continue to receive calls and emails and even invoices for services rendered. You may have even signed something along the way (in the fine print that you didn't read) that gave them the right to do so. Your failure to pay will be reported to credit agencies and you will be left with the decision to pay up or face the consequences of a lowered credit rating.

You may find it hard to believe that these "nice consultants" are often big fat liars. They are adept at convincing you that they are your best chance of getting your product to market. They seem to be your best buddy, but in reality, they're your worst nightmare, as they know that you'll never make a dime, and they probably couldn't care less. For these consultants, it's all about the commission and they receive a commission (from the payments you make) whether or not you ever sell a single unit. **Remember: Most fee-based invention**

marketing companies are scams.

In a recent interview with Josh Malone, inventor of *Bunch O Balloons* he shares this: "I've been hearing from inventors about the licensing deals they struck recently and I ask, 'Wow! Well, how much did they give you? You got a $5,000 advance, right?' "No. Nothing.' I then ask them, 'What's your royalty?' 2% is what I normally hear. 'When are they going to pay you?' I ask. 'I don't know.'"

Josh goes on to say, "I've also learned that many of the agreements the inventors are offered are not actually licensing agreements but rather, test agreements which typically last anywhere from three months to a year (even though they are called licensing agreements). This is done so that invention submission companies are able to comply with regulations that require them to report their success rates) that they helped inventors get a licensing deal when actually, it is nothing more than a no-obligation test agreement."

One client, a disabled veteran (we will call him John Thomas) submitted a concept for a car product to an invention submission company he saw advertising on TV. They created a promotional video, a sales sheet, and designed a logo (charging him thousands of dollars to do so). He then began receiving emails naming target companies that they'd approach for licensing deals. For each sales pitch, the company charged $395.00. This went on for years. John Thomas was never given any feedback as to why companies turned him down – feedback that may have been valuable in terms of evaluating the marketability of his product. Instead, on a regular basis, he'd receive company's sales pitches encouraging him to continue with the company because "they try longer." Clearly, the longer they try, the more money they get in *their* pocket.

By the time an invention submission company is done

with you (meaning you're broke and can't pay them anything else to continue to do nothing for you), you will likely have spent $15,000 or more with them with very little to show for it and no money-back for the unsatisfied customer (unless you want to go to arbitration).

If you have been scammed by an invention submission company, you can make a complaint to your local Attorney General's Office, or the Federal Trade Commission. If you are unsure as to whether an invention promoter is committing fraud, the United States Patent Office will post any complaints on their website, together with any responses they do receive at:

https://www.uspto.gov/patents-getting-started/using-legal-services/scam-prevention/published-complaints/published.

The Randy Cooper Foundation is also another resource that can help you research and track down scam companies (or illegal bootleggers).

I also know of several inventors that have "trusted" sites that ask you to allow them to post your product on their site publicly, in order to garner interest from distributors. The problem with allowing them to disclose your idea publicly is that it puts you at risk (even if you have already filed for your intellectual property rights). People are trolling every day looking on these sites for new ideas, and if you publicly disclose your idea, well, you open yourself to infringement before you even have the chance to get it to market yourself.

The next thing you know, you are seeking a licensing deal, and what you thought you had protected by a provisional patent, or other protection, shows up out of nowhere on QVC, Amazon or Walmart, and leaves you wondering, "How in the hell did that happen so fast?" Well, it was easy; you opened the door when you allowed a company to publicly display your product idea on their sites.

Invention Submission companies make money because they assure you that your product has huge potential (they never put this in writing; however, they will tell you this during one of their multiple phone calls where they cheer you on and ask you for more money). They convince you that companies are just all over their site looking for the next "Big Idea" and that idea could be YOURS. Well, nine times out of ten, they are lying to you, because a lot of people trolling their sites as well as crowdfunding sites (such as Kickstarter) are people looking to steal your intellectual property!

A VISION FOR YOU

If you have an invention, guard it like you would your own baby. You'd probably not leave your baby with a stranger whom you met via a website, so why treat your product-baby that way? There are some good advisors out there though, do your best to get a personal recommendation prior to engaging them. Moreover, paying $99.00 or more to a company to enable you to fill out your provisional patent application online is $99.00 wasted. You can find these forms online for free, but if you don't know how to draft patent claims, you are simply wasting your time (and money) because your application will be rejected.

Somewhere between 2% and 10% of all patents have ever made money. However, if you hire an invention promoter, your chances of success could be closer to zero. They will likely never tell you, for example, that you need to file a utility patent after your provisional patent expires in one year. Why? Because if your product is a hit, and your patent expires, it's fair game for any of their feeder companies who will produce your product and you will never know how that happened. When you try to enforce your patent rights, you come to find out that your patent is expired. Game Over.

Be smart and perform your own due diligence when hiring any individual or company. Just type into "Google Search" – the name of the person or corporation you're investigating and then include: + complaints + fraud + lawsuits. You'll be amazed at what's there. Also, don't forget to check out the patent lawyers at the USPTO – and make sure that they're "registered" and in "good standing."

Performing an Internet search on invention submission company is simply not enough because either (1) they pay for fake reviews that tout their excellence or pay to have negative comments removed from sites (such as Ripoffreport.com); or (2) they settle with disgruntled clients in exchange for the inventor agreeing never to speak a word of it again or they will be subject to a lawsuit.

Meanwhile, as a precaution – just ask any invention promoter to show you a copy of **a real royalty check** from a verifiable manufacturer or distributor– and after that – you'll never hear from them again.

Not all product babies are beautiful. But, even the ugliest product babies can grow up to be beautiful children. Product babies must be cared for and nurtured in a way that makes them appealing to a broad group of potential buyers. At its core, inventorship is the process of education; learning lessons that, when applied correctly, can help determine whether you can turn your baby into a beautiful product without taking it in the kadoodle in the process.

Personally, we are not going to tell you whether or not we think you have a great product, and any lawyer, consultant or invention help company who tries to tell you that they think your product is great is simply trying to schmooze you to sell you their services. In speaking with successful marketers, we've asked them, "Why do you think this product failed?" The most common is response was that "no one has a crystal ball. Some products can test very well and we end up losing money in the end, and others can test poorly and then surprise us." But, I can tell you this - it doesn't take a crystal ball to predict that if you surround yourself with people who understand the industry and are honest and trustworthy - whether or not you have a good product - you are going to either succeed or avoid spending needless dollars on unnecessary services to develop a product that won't ever end up on a retail shelf.

Guest Contribution:
3 Keys to Inventing Successful New Products™
Authored by Eric P. Rose, NPDP, MBA

>TACTICS, TIPS & MORE >>PAGES 127 - 130

YOU'LL SAY WOW
EVERY TIME

2

The best things in life are free - and $19.95 - Billy Mays

A great business pitch is among the first of many skills an entrepreneur must hone to get their concept off the ground. Whether you're raising capital or selling a product online, people have many choices so, why would they choose to invest in you or your product?

Countless inventors have blown an opportunity because they didn't "wow" their audience. You don't have to be a big-shot speaker like Tony Robbins to wow your audience - you simply need to be engaging and get your message across with clarity, confidence, and conviction as no one knows your vision better than you. However, once the "fish" is on the hook, it is the reeling in part where many inventors fall short, particularly in the DRTV industry.

DRTV stands for "Direct Response Television" and refers to any television (or digital) advertising that asks consumers to either visit a website or call an 800 number to make a purchase. Frequently, the product offering is coupled with other "exclusive offers"; products which are known as "upsells," and they normally include some sort of "money back" guarantees. DRTV products are typically sold at a price point of $19.99 plus shipping and handling. [SIDE NOTE: The "money back" guarantee enables you to return the product for the full price you paid less shipping and handling.]

When you think about highly successful *As Seen on TV* products like *OxiClean®*, *Chia Pet®*, *ShamWow®*, *PedEgg®*, and *Snuggie®*, while all very different products, they all have one very thing in common: They were all sold to consumers using DRTV. Now, all these products have become household names, and you can buy them in the stores or online. As an inventor, you probably dream of one day seeing your product on TV, whether on *Shark Tank* or on 30-60-second commercials (typically called "Short Form Ads") or on 30-60-minute commercials (typically called "Long Form Ads"), or on television shopping channels, such as QVC, HSN, or Shop NBC.

Achieving this dream takes a lot of guts and determination and, yes, money! Toward the end of the inventing cycle, after developing prototype after prototype until it's been perfected, and after paying to draft and file your patent and copyrights, unless you have just cashed in a winning lottery ticket, in all likelihood, you have exhausted much of your bank account. Nonetheless, since you have come too far to throw in the towel, even if you have started to doubt yourself or the potential of your idea, this is time for you to exert your confidence. To borrow a quote from Thomas Edison, "Nearly every man who develops an idea works it up to the point where it looks impossible, and then he gets discouraged. That's not the place to become discouraged." As an inventor, you simply need to fake it till you make it (I don't know who to credit that quote to, but it's a good one!).

A couple years back, I was referred by a client to a new

inventor (we'll call him Ray); this client provides a great example of how a deal can be blown by desperate behavior.

Ray and I began working together immediately, and we chose a very reputable DRTV company from his list of potential "suitors" to license his product. The company was excited and sent over their letter of intent which contained standard terms including an advance payment, a reasonable royalty clause, and a commitment to purchase a minimum quantity in the first year (typically, 250,000 - 500,000 units). In the course of negotiations, we sent back a few edits to the agreement. Without giving the company time to review, Ray let his desperate flag fly and emailed the company each day for the rest of the week asking when the contract could be signed. I begged Ray to give it a few days to avoid scaring them off. In a Hail Mary, Ray emailed them a final note: "We are broke, flat broke. We are on food stamps for about 6 months now. I need this signed."

The company emailed back later that day to say, "After a second round of analysis and internal deliberations, we have concluded that we must pass on the opportunity to license and market your product."

Long story short, the lesson here is that - unless you have invented a product that either cures cancer or eliminates world hunger - **no one** will ever want it badly enough to partner with someone who appears unstable or desperate. You also have to remember that product marketers are probably evaluating and negotiating with multiple inventors at the same time, so as much as you want to sign the deal, some patience will be required during the negotiation process.

My daughter's friend, Nicole, was on pins and needles waiting for her college acceptance letter. Imagine if she decided to call and email the school every day to ask for an update on her status? Similarly, you'd likely not apply for a job and then harass the hiring manager every day for an answer. The same rule applies here, folks.

* * * *

Francesca Kuglen, an inventor, entrepreneur, women's advocate and the CEO of *HairZing®*, is by all standards, a seasoned entrepreneur. She started her first company fresh out of college with $250 and sold it 11 years later to Rubbermaid.

In 2009, Francesca was looking for a solution to keep her hair up. She wanted to use double-combs, but nothing like that existed on the market so, she invented it. She filed a patent application for a fashionable double-hair comb that allows you to create multiple styles and trademarked the name, *HairZing®*. When she tried to license it, she was told that it was too complicated -- that no one could understand the hair accessory. Not one to be discouraged, Francesca decided to go it alone and built a company. After getting the product on QVC, it was a huge success; it generated a couple of million in sales right away. Unbeknownst to her, the QVC spot was seen by a very large infomercial company and low and behold, they came out with a product that was *so similar* that even her own mother couldn't tell the products apart. She tried to fight the bad guys (using some unorthodox methods at first) and ultimately ended up in court. The lawsuit drained her company and her lifesavings; she finally was forced to settle. As her patent was still pending at the time, her insurance company thought the case too "high-risk" to support. Today, she has established a successful relationship with Conair and her Hairzing® products are on the shelves countrywide in Target and other leading retail stores.

Sipping coffee at her favorite Oakland café, Francesca speaks with authority, passion and a contagious sense of humor:

"Many companies are looking for inventors with great products they can quickly take to market... But can you show them you're a normal rational person? The bottom line is that distributors are afraid of crazy-ass inventors that ask, for example, 'I want a $1,000,000 signing bonus.'" Kuglen puts down her latte, looks me firmly in the eyes and warns, "People working in their basements who are undercapitalized and desperate are bound to destroy themselves, their families, and all that is good and holy in their lives if they don't get themselves some professional help."

While inventors who have put everything on the line to launch their product are obviously under a great deal of financial pressure, the stress that they feel can come across as desperate. No one can negotiate from a position of strength when they are in a position of desperation. Being desperate can also put you at the greatest risk for negotiating a bad deal or worse yet, having your product stolen from you (e.g., by eagerly sharing your patent drawings or other confidential information with unscrupulous people).

Negotiating is uncomfortable for many people. Standing up for yourself, asking for what you want, and trying to get a better price or, terms and conditions often feels confrontational–and most non-lawyers prefer to avoid confrontation. Distributors and licensing companies understand that you are uncomfortable in asking for what you want and have been known to take advantage of this. In short, you need to learn how to "wow" your prospective business partners and customers and then be cool about it. Be willing to walk away if you are not comfortable with the deal.

Perhaps the best place to practice your negotiating skills is at a flea market or yard sale where the stakes are relatively low. It's a great place for exploring the effectiveness of different approaches and documenting what worked and what didn't work (e.g., what resulted in sales and what resulted in the potential buyer saying "thanks, but no thanks").

If anyone has a knack for making a pitch, it's Vince Offer – infamously known as the *ShamWow*® Guy. Renowned for his upbeat, smooth-talking humorous scripts, Vince honed his pitches by going to flea markets, such as the Rose Bowl, and trying out different sales techniques. He has produced highly successful infomercials, including the *ShamWow*!® which has become a cult classic. Vince is also well-known in industry circles for the *SlapChop*® and *Schticky*®.

A great infomercial has the effect of making the viewer feel like that new amazing product gizmo does everything but cure the common hangover and you've got to have it now! But wait … there's more, if you act now, you will get another one *absolutely free.*

And, if you want that stuff to show up at your front door faster than you can say *Sham-Wow*, simply pay for rush shipping. Cha-ching!

Successful pitchmen also recommend that you keep a notebook or make notes on your smartphone of the feedback you receive so you can refer back later on and continue to refine your pitch. Once you have mastered your pitch you then have to impress upon them why they have got to have it *now*.

Ron Popeil, renowned for his catchy humorous scripts, also honed his pitches by going to flea markets and demonstrating products at Woolworth's department store. Most famous for the *Ronco Spray Gun*® and the *Chop-O-Matic*®, in the 1950s, he brought his pitch to TV, becoming an icon of the infomercial world and popularizing catch phrases such as, "But wait, there's more..." and "Operators are standing by...".

Another great pitch commonly used in infomercials is encouraging the buyer to "ACT NOW" because the offer will either expire or the supply is limited. For example, in addition to offering a buy-one-get-one promotion, pitchmen also group a number of products together (e.g., a $9.99 vegetable peeler and a $19.99 veggie slicer can be yours for just $15.99.) Multiple offers will often increase your negotiating leverage (and your profits).

When experienced pitchmen launch new products, distributors line up to be the first ones to exclusively test and market their products. This is because these pitchmen have a proven success record, and with a proven success record comes confidence. With confidence comes the ability to negotiate with anyone - from your manufacturer to your distributor to the retailer who will place your product on their shelves.

Always keep in mind that you are not only selling a product, but selling yourself as well. As the infamous Billy Mays (notable for his promotion of *OxiClean®, Orange Glo®, Kaboom®*, and other cleaning products), once stated, "Life's a pitch ... and then you buy." So, hone your pitch and make a good impression if you want to see your product on TV or on a retail shelf someday.

TOP TAKEWAYS

- *Never beg someone to buy your product; there are plenty of options, you need to find the best fit.*

- *Your financial status (or other personal info) is no one's concern; don't use that information as a negotiating tool.*

- *Watch videos (YouTube) and infomercials to see how others pitch their product. Practice with friends, family, and advisors to get it right.*

- *Hone your sales skills, figure out what works and what doesn't before presenting your product to potential buyers.*

- *Work with a TRUSTED advisor or mentor who can provide guidance.*

- *Be patient - Never rush a company to make a decision for what could be a life-changing deal for you.*

- *Be professional - a company is not just buying a product; they are buying into your dream.*

- *No one is going to do business with a crazy person - don't let your emotions cloud your judgment.*

3

THEY DON'T CALL IT *SHARK TANK* FOR NOTHING

If you really look closely, most overnight successes took a long time. - Steve Jobs

For those of you inventors who haven't heard of *Shark Tank*, it is the leading reality TV show where inventors compete to appear on the show to pitch their product and (hopefully) walk away with a lucrative investment or distribution deal. More common than not, their products and pitches end up being ripped to shreds by the sharp teeth of the judges (successful entrepreneurs such as Mark Cuban or Barbara Cochrane). They may walk away empty-handed, but hopefully, take away from the experience some advice as to what the inventor needs to do differently in order to be successful. In any event, it is good exposure and, may prove to be good publicity to drive buyers to your website.

Inventors, today, are all clamoring to get on this industry specific reality show for their 15 minutes of fame. Though, *Shark Tank* is appropriately named because when you embark on the business of inventing and selling your product, you are quite literally swimming with the "Sharks." The most successful marketing and distribution companies – including Telebrands,

Allstar, TriStar and Emson – to name a few of the most elite - have negotiated thousands of licensing contracts, and their revenues are in the billions. They think fast and they talk even faster, and their ability to negotiate deals on behalf of their companies has catapulted them into a league of their own. From "*Snuggies*," to *ShamWow*! to *Bunch O Balloons*, to *Gotham Steel*, and *Red Copper* pans – they are all responsible for the bulk of the products you see advertised on TV, on home shopping channels, or on the shelves of Target or Walmart.

If you are thinking to yourself, "WOW! this is great information, let me Google these companies and submit my ideas to one of *them*," good for you for having such passion! If you are thinking to yourself that the thought of negotiating with any of these leading marketers intimidates the crap out of you, good for you for keeping it real.

Whether or not you actually have a "hit" product is not for me or any of the "Sharks" to say. You should also be wary of anyone who is trying to sell you a service that will help you launch your product and/or get you a distribution deal for an upfront fee. This is because they have an inherent conflict of interest – they are happy to take your money even if your product (1) is not unique (e.g., it has been done before); (2) does not have a big enough market to generate considerable profits; or (3) is too costly to manufacture. Consulting a product coach is useful in terms of understanding whether your product has potential. There are also plenty of inventor-mentors who are happy to share their experiences (at no cost to you) to steer you in the right direction.

A SHARK'S TALE

Guest Submission
Tracy Hazzard, CEO of Hazz Design, Podcast Host, Brand Strategist.

Shelly Ehler is an inspiring entrepreneur and the inventor of the *ShowNo towel*. Her towel has also been featured on *The TODAY Show*, *The View*, and *Good Morning America*. She was featured on Season 3 of *Shark Tank*, and her product and presentation were such a hit that she had three "Sharks" fighting over her. Shelly is the only entrepreneur in the show's history to ever leave with a check in her hand from Lori Greiner. Ehler had been hand-sewing her towels, borrowing to prepare for what she thought would be the ride of a lifetime, and felt like she was patiently waiting on the verge of success she had been dreaming about as she poured blood, sweat, and tears into her business. Then she went on *Shark Tank* and was handed a check! Sounds like the ultimate *Shark Tank* success... right? Wrong!

"Don't cash that check," Ehler was told following the show. However, that was not the call Shelly was expecting to receive from Lori Greiner. Shelly's mouth hung open as Greiner listed her concerns on the other end of the line. "Your business is too new, the deal we made isn't the deal I want to make now...blah, blah." As Ehler listened to the words that were her new reality, she could feel the anxiety and stress wash over her. Entrepreneurship can be full of angst, desperation, and a constant stream of a steady inner voices asking you if you're worthy enough to "be here." In that moment, those very same entrepreneurial fears planted firmly in Ehler's mind because she put her trust in a "Shark." But "Sharks" prey on eager bait, and this story isn't the only one where we can see the damaging effects of *Shark Tank* on entrepreneurs and inventors who are just trying to make their dreams come true for themselves, and their families.

"Whatever you think," said Shelly. The new deal on the table offered Ehler a 70/30 split, with the latter being her percentage. In her gut, she knew this deal wasn't fair, but she was met with aggression when she spoke out. When she started asking me questions like, "Do you know what I can do for you?" or, "Do you know how much I charge for my time?" Then, she followed that up with statements like, "Shelly, I am going to do this for you; I went all in."

The other offers that the other "Sharks" made to Ehler on the show were now off the table, but she was under the impression, based on conversations with Greiner, that the *ShowNo Towel* was going to make them millions. When she looked at everything from this angle, Ehler felt like maybe she could live with a 30% deal. So, with a nod and a few famous last words, "Whatever you think," she sealed the fate of her towel. And then things went even further downhill, and ultimately, her *ShowNo Towel* was a no-show in revenues and eventually, went out of business.

The thing that a lot of people don't realize is that those "Sharks" aren't there to promote the entrepreneur and make the entrepreneur money. The "Sharks" are there to promote *themselves, their businesses, their business acumen*, and to solidify *their business legacy*. The guests on the show, the inventors and creators, are just part of that plan. I think viewers believe *Shark Tank* is the embodiment of the American Dream, but if we take a closer look, we can see that the show is more the embodiment of self-promotion, greed, and a "whatever it takes" type of attitude, no matter who gets hurt in the process - basically, it's entertainment at the inventor's expense.

Stories like Ehler's make me cringe because the minute

she took that deal, she was at the mercy of someone who was using her and her life's work to self-promote, and at any cost. Just like with Ehler, it is very common for the deals made on the show to fall through. When you watch, you just assume that those deals that they air are the deals that *actually* happen, and oftentimes, that just isn't the case, once the camera stops rolling.

It's so much easier to take innovation (as in EXPLOIT) than it is to innovate; which is one of the biggest reasons why I am weary of any reality show, or "opportunity" like *Shark Tank*, where innovators - eager to grow their business - expose their products (oftentimes without patent, trademark, or copyright protection) and end up as shark bait.

Over the years, I've had several clients who were featured on *Shark Tank*, made a deal with a "Shark", and then their deal fell through... not quite "As Seen on TV" as we might think. Sometimes, as a result of the airing of the show, viewers flock to the website to place orders. So, while customer demand was created, without funding from a "Shark", they can't source or fulfill the orders unless they are going to do so from their garage. It is a soul-crushing experience. I hate it! Business and entrepreneurship, and neither is for the faint of heart, but at the same time, can we go on condoning abuse, greed, and predatory behavior?

Everything is so soft and lovely on television – even when the "Sharks" are ripping their prey apart, there's a bit of humor and the entrepreneur seemingly leaves in one piece. Off the air, there's no softness, there's no editing, there's no producer creating perfect dialogue, or heartfelt moments, or scenarios where participants leave with a check in their hand because the newest "Shark" on the show needs to appeal to a specific target audience to sell her current products and businesses.

"I'm part of an exclusive and prestigious club," Greiner tells a pair of female entrepreneurs. "I'm a woman" (as though she is going all out to join the sisterhood of the traveling pants). And, just like that, we can see how easily "Sharks" can manipulate the wide-eyed show participants with all the feel-good, hoorah type of attitude that TV allows.

Off the air, businesses are crushed because, rather than putting an expert in their tank, they chose a "Shark." Statistically, in the marketplace, you're more likely to fail than you are to succeed, and that depends on your definition of success.

- *14 out of 15 HSN and QVC products fail to make money and/or fail in the marketplace.*[1]

- *7 out of 10 consumer products fail in the marketplace.*[2]

I have an 86% success rate, and when you look at statistics like this side-by-side, it's easy to see why it makes more sense to seek out an expert in your product or service area, versus taking such massive risks to appear on reality television for your friends and family to see. It isn't that *Shark Tank* is all bad. Plenty of businesses are still running, plenty of deals actually go through, plenty of entrepreneurs live to tell about their swim with the "Sharks"… but I can tell you this right now – it isn't what you think, it isn't what it looks like, it doesn't happen overnight, and it isn't all rainbows and unicorns. What you see on TV is one very minuscule piece of one very large puzzle

Some contestants get the writing on the wall much quicker in the process, and are able to swim away before there is blood in the water. Kiersten Parsons Hathcock, TV network executive turned self-taught carpenter and furniture designer,

1   Cory Bergeron - http://corybergeron.com/
2   Why Most Product Launches Fail, Harvard Business Review (April 2011) https://hbr.org/2011/04/why-most-product-launches-fail.

won a deal on ABC's *Shark Tank* in 2010. Her furniture company, *Mod Mom*, captured Robert Herjavec's attention, and after her pitch, she patiently awaited his call. When the call finally came, like Shelly, it certainly wasn't the one she was expecting either. Herjavec's change of heart, citing her business still being too small, left her reeling.

Luckily, Hathcock had family and friends who were able to invest; however, a lot of entrepreneurs are not in this fortunate position, and a lost opportunity, like the one *Mod Mom* suffered, is the end of the road. She was able to keep going on her own, and her furniture line was recently picked up by Little Colorado.

Another entrepreneur who experienced a similar bait and switch scenario with Herjavec was Megan Cummins, who went in the tank to pitch *You Smell*, her luxury soap company. On the show, Herjavec offered Cummins investment in exchange for 20% of her company, but when he sent her the contract, he was asking for 50% of her business, for the same investment amount. Cummins, reeling from the bait and switch, turned the deal down, and was able to sell her business in 2014. After selling *You Smell*, Cummins launched *Sparklepop* and is on track to be one of the fastest growing small businesses in the States.

As previous contestant Jordan Scott puts it, in his book, *Shark Bites*, "There is nothing else on Earth like being in the tank." This is true for multiple reasons. First, the process of getting a fair and sensible valuation on the show is not in any way how valuations are done in the real world. Second, you would never sit in a room with potential investors and be devalued in the manner of which we see on the show. Oftentimes, investors aren't looking for the check marks that the "Sharks" make sticking points about on the show, and in a lot of ways, this kind of false representation of how business actually works, is damaging, especially for new entrepreneurs who are learning it all as they go. Third, I've had a handful of clients who got deals on *Shark Tank*, and were in no way ready to make those deals, but nobody told them that.

When you don't have the experience to know what's missing, and you don't have the systems and processes in place to take advantage of the swell of growth that could potentially be coming your way, it's easy to take missteps; creating unnecessary vulnerabilities and taking unnecessary risks. This might not seem like a big deal to a "Shark" with a portfolio that is bursting at the seams, but for these entrepreneurs, this is their livelihood, their baby, their everything… they've emptied bank accounts, they've taken loans, and they've borrowed from friends and family. When the dust settles, it isn't the "Sharks" who look those people in the eye, it isn't the "Sharks" who repay those loans at exorbitant interest rates, and it isn't the "Sharks" who nurse the wounds. With all of that being said, let's take a look at the **top 5 signs that you are ready for the tank:**

- *You have market proof and traction. Do you have a reachable market? Can you show who your competition is and how you're different? Do you have quantifiable data? You must be able to show your traction in the marketplace.*

- *You are profitable. Entrepreneurs don't need to have a million dollars in sales to be ready for Shark Tank, but you do need to show solid profitability or the immediate potential for profit.*

- *You know your hook. A perfect pitch is one that is clear, speaks to the unique elements of a business, and has a hook to really grab the attention of listeners.*

- **You know your numbers.** It is cringeworthy to watch episodes where entrepreneurs don't know their numbers because, as an entrepreneur, you should know this information like the back of your hand, no excuses. If you don't know your numbers, you are putting yourself in a very vulnerable position because, how can you ask for your value if you don't know your numbers? And how can you realistically pitch a plan for profitability, if you don't know your margins?

- **You have a plan.** If you know your plan for the future, have a vision for the business, and can show long-term potential in an investment, this is a great indicator of preparedness and sustainability.

If you can read through these readiness signs and know, without a doubt, that you can check each box, you might be in a position to join the other 45,000 annual applications for *Shark Tank*. But I have to ask, if you can check these boxes, why aren't you protecting your business and going it alone? If you have a foundation to launch, why not launch where you are, build your business organically, and control the process each step of the way?

So many entrepreneurs think the other entrepreneurs have more knowledge or more access, but I can tell you that (for the most part) everyone is just out there hustling and figuring it out, day in, and day out. When I go back and watch Ehler's pitch to the "Sharks," it kills me when she gets a check on the spot. I find myself talking to the screen, "Don't take the check...don't take the check." "This is a huge red flag." In Ehler's mind, it proved out her worth; however, in hindsight, it's clear that if someone is willing to hand you a check on the spot, your business is probably worth more.

192 sleepless nights, anxious energy, and not speak-

ing to a soul about the fact that she might be on *Shark Tank* were torture for Ehler. But finally, her episode aired… and then nothing happened. Ehler and I talked about lessons learned, entrepreneurship, and how her vulnerability and excitement were used against her in an effort to take her business out from underneath her.

"The last offer Greiner made me was a royalty deal. My attorney said it was one of the worst he'd ever seen and it would have left me with nothing. At that point, I knew it was time to walk away, and at least keep what was left of my pride. I couldn't help but take it personally and I felt like the biggest failure. Now that I've had some time to heal and get a better perspective, I see a lot more. I don't think [Lori] ever had any intention of letting me have that money. She was new on the show, wanted to make a splash, and I felt the check hand-off was a production-value stunt to help her make a name for herself. When the dust settled, I really had nothing left, and it took me 3-years to come back and start rebuilding with a renewed vision."

Of course, Ehler isn't the only one. There are entire Facebook "support" groups, hiding in the shadows, dedicated solely to building some sort of common-ground comradery to help heal the wounds of those who suffered "Shark" bites. But too many victims don't speak up because they haven't even begun the healing process. When you go up against a "Shark" (or an entire tank full of them), nothing can prepare you, no matter how much you tell yourself otherwise, to be ripped to shreds, to have your creation ripped to shreds, to be manipulated, and preyed upon. Nothing is going to help ease the anxiety and the voice that questions your worthiness. No one is going to hold your hand, and help you navigate the murky waters… but hey, if things get really bad, there is a show therapist who might offer some couch time.

There are two really common misconceptions about *Shark Tank* that I want to debunk as I close this out. One, you have to know that the show is not for the entrepreneur. The show is for the promotion of the "Sharks," their portfolios, and their brands. I know I mentioned this, but I really want you to think about this the next time you find yourself settling in for an episode of *Shark Tank*. This perspective shift will change the way you watch, feel, and perceive the show, as well as the "Sharks".

Secondly, a "Shark" *is not going to launch your product or business for you*. Plenty of entrepreneurs, or even viewers, have this idea that being "seen" on TV is a magic bullet, but it isn't. If any part of your potential success dream is resting on this misconception, you really should consider talking to a product launch expert to get a more realistic idea of how this process really works. Episode after episode, I've seen these points hammered home, and this just proves that the show isn't a full story and totally honest depiction of the possibilities. The entrepreneurs and creators I meet oftentimes have this vision of quality and building something that feels like an extension of their values, world view, and passion for impact. I wish more entrepreneurs would commit to that vision and stay the course. Slow and steady really does win the race. I believe "Sharks" attempt to remove the entrepreneur (along with some integrity) from the process to force fit it into their brand or their system. Next time your best friend from college tells you that you should go on *Shark Tank* because you'd be *totally perfect for that*, ask her how she feels about swimming alone in murky water with a bunch of sharks while playing the movie, *Jaws*, in the background.

****

Tiffany Krumins, who refers to herself as an "accidental entrepreneur", had an entirely different experience with *Shark Tank* and one that catapulted her into a successful entrepreneur with the help of a "Shark", Barbara Corcoran. Tiffany worked as a caregiver for a boy with Downs Syndrome. He had a difficult time taking medication; so much so that he had to be restrained in order to take even the smallest of pills. She had a lightbulb moment - he loves stuffed animals so, why not incorporate that into the medicine-taking routine? That night she went home and took different materials and created an elephant out of sponges and fabrics and fitted the inside with recordable greeting card. She recorded her voice on the card as a talking elephant. When she took it to work the next day, she said,

"Gibby, this is your little buddy. She is going to help you take your medicine today." At the moment, something just clicked with him; it was as if he was never fearful of medicine. He listened to this elephant's soothing directions and took his medicine. With that aha-ha moment came the next thought: "What do I do to make this available to kids everywhere?"

About six months later, Tiffany saw a casting call for *Shark Tank*. It was the pilot episode of the show and the casting read, "Do you have the next big million-dollar idea but you don't have the funding to make it happen?" She submitted her idea and, one week later, she was accepted on the pilot episode of *Shark Tank*. After signing the deal with Barbara, Tiffany was thrust into the product launch world -- everything from designing and filing her trademark and patent and designing packaging to negotiating with manufacturers. While Barbara was extremely supportive, her background was in real estate so, this was her first product launch, too. Although there were bumps and hiccups along the way, Barbara profited from her gamble on *Ava the Elephant*® and eight years from her ah-ha moment, Tiffany succeeded in obtaining a lucrative licensing deal. Most recently, Tiffany branched out and launched Mom Genius which aims to combine the excitement of *Shark Tank* with access to genius, kid-inspired products and to nurture other inventors.

So, folks, there are always tales of woe and tales of success in product launching, even though the success stories don't happen overnight. *Shark Tank* has evolved quite a bit from the original pilot episode to the big hit reality show it is today and even those that walk off the show as a winner may still find themselves swimming the backstroke as, the Sharks don't always deliver on the promises they make on national TV.

"Dude, you'll need a bigger boat, because you're going to sell 75,000 units overnight when you swim with the sharks!"

A FOOL
FOR A CLIENT

4

An entrepreneur tends to bite off a little more than he can chew hoping he'll quickly learn how to chew it - **Roy Ash**

My grandmother has a saying, "Never get good at the things you don't like doing." On Grandma's advice, I never learned how to properly iron a shirt, mop a floor, or put the down-blanket back inside the duvet cover. While I have clearly used this advice throughout my life in a self-serving manner, it's true that, unless we enjoy something or have the skill set, experience, or training to handle a particular task, in all likelihood, we are not going to be very good at it. Similarly, from filing your own patents to negotiating your own licensing deals, unless you have the skill set (and, I don't mean you simply "buy a book, watch a video or attend a workshop), don't do it.

You have probably all heard the expression, "A lawyer who defends himself has a fool for a client." This is true for a few reasons. First, the "law" is a huge body of knowledge. I specialize in intellectual property and contracts. If I had to go to probate court to contest a will or go to family court to file for divorce, I would find someone who specializes in the field of the law that will best help my case. Another reason why it's helpful to hire an experienced advocate is that it is hard for anyone to be objective when emotions run high. With clouded judgment, it is difficult to make rational decisions. An attorney - someone without the emotional investment – can help us make more objective decisions than we could otherwise ourselves.

But, what about the inventor who represents himself or herself? Inventors, by nature, are emotionally invested in their products. They may have spent years thinking, tweaking, and perfecting a design. They have likely spent a lot of money prototyping, patenting, and even developing product marketing materials to promote their idea. Inventing, like the law, is a specialization and, unless you are a serial inventor - with several successful products under your belt - you'll want to find someone who specializes in patent drafting, sales, distribution, and digital marketing. You'd also want to hire a lawyer who understands the ins and outs of manufacturing, licensing, and related industry agreements.

Analyzing contracts is a specialty. For example, non-lawyers think that when they read a word, it means something, but in a legal context, it can mean something radically different. The nature of our legal system is that it depends heavily on precedent. That is, the outcome in a current case is determined by reference to the outcome in prior cases. Case outcomes influence contract drafting. For example, under New York case law unless a contract specifically states that a prevailing party in a case is entitled to legal fees (or a statute exists that allows for an award of legal fees) no legal fees will be awarded. In addition, words, phrases, and terms included in a contract are given meanings that are developed in lines of cases. Thus, so-called "legalese," while usually used as a denigrating label, is in fact the technical language of the law. Each type of contract - be it real estate, wills and trusts, or investment documents - all rely on different precedent and therefore, will all have its own technical language.

There are a few clauses in a distribution or licensing contract that really (and I mean REALLY!) make the difference of *whether you will ever see a dime of your royalties* and *whether you can cancel the agreement* if you don't. This chapter is intended to shed some light on a few of the most critical clauses that pose the biggest problems (and confusion) in distribution or licensing deals.

TEST AGREEMENTS

Many distribution contracts start with a Test Agreement, meaning the distributor will ask for a 6-month exclusive right to test your product to see whether there is interest. They will develop marketing materials, buy media (such a Facebook and Instagram ads) and test your product at different price points to various target markets. Determining whether your product tested successfully is measured by a MER score. MER stands for Marketing Expense Ratio. This means that for every dollar spent on advertising, a marketer is looking to double their money. In other words, if they spent $10,000 on advertising and then sell $20,000 in goods, you'd receive a 2:1 MER score, which is considered a successful test. Another measurement is called a conversion rate. Let's say they marketed to 100 customers, which resulted in 20 sales. Your sales-to-lead conversion rate would be 20%, which is also a very desirable result. If – for whatever reason - the distributor decides not to enter into a distribution contract, you will nonetheless want to request a copy of the Test Results. Test Results are not something automatically given, and it must be negotiated as part of your Test Agreement. With these results in hand, you are in a better position to move straight to a distribution deal with another suitor, particularly, if the results looked promising.

ADJUSTED GROSS REVENUE OR REVENUE CLAUSES

This clause contains the amount of royalty percentage you receive based on net profits. Net profits are gross profits, less costs. Every distribution agreement includes a laundry list of costs that a licensor will attempt to deduct from the gross profit number to essentially reduce the amount of money you will receive. Oftentimes, these costs are vague and over-reaching. For example, it is generally acceptable for net sales to include deductions for shipping freight, taxes, credits, and returns. It is not desirable to include deductions for sales commissions, debts, uncollectable accounts, promotions, marketing, and advertising.

I spend more time negotiating this clause than any other term in an agreement. This is the MONEY clause, people. Each company will have its own version of what would be considered very one-sided language that - **spoiler alert** - does not favor you!

A client (we'll call her Sarah) invented a new design for a blanket. She retained me to review her contract with a company we'll call Greedy Company, Inc. ("Greedy" for short). She told me, "I need to get this deal signed or I will jump off of the Golden Gate Bridge." I told her that if she signed the deal as is, I'd want to join her on that bridge!

The Greedy contract serves as perfect example of the type of licensing agreement that you do not want to sign. In fact, you'd be better off going it alone, rather than binding yourself to the terms that were proposed to Sarah.

So, let's delve in here! Greedy offered Sarah 5% of the net sales from their sale of her product. Their standard contract reads as follows:

Net Sales – Net Sales shall be defined as gross revenue from the product (the amount the product sold for by Greedy excluding shipping and handling and upsells) less the following: purchase price of the product (including landed duties paid), chargebacks, returns, allowances, cash and trade discounts, sales commissions, credit card discounts, bad checks and charges for bad checks, all of Greedy's out-of-pocket costs associated with the product, including but not limited to the cost to advertise and distribute the product (including all media purchases), customer service charge, website development (and costs associated with maintaining the product's website), agency fees, commissions, fulfillments, shipping, and an administrative overhead fee in the amount equal to seven percent (7%) of the gross revenue.

When reading this clause for the first time, I felt as if I was reading the warning label of a pharmaceutical product! Based on this language, it would be impossible for anyone to do an audit to ensure that the royalty payments you were offered were fair, as there was no insight into agency fees, commissions, fulfillment, etc. What if Greedy decided to spend $100,000 on her website? As you can see, when a distributor attempts to include everything but the kitchen sink in their deductions, that raises a major red flag. How can you ever be certain that the royalties you are receiving are correct if there are so many unknown costs associated with selling your product?

So, I deleted out the entire clause and replaced it instead with, "*Licensor shall receive $1.00 per unit for each unit sold.*"

Not all companies will be receptive to this approach; from my experience, many reputable companies are willing to offer you a fixed-dollar figure rather than a percentage of "net sales." Failing that, reputable companies will NEVER attempt to deduct marketing or advertising expenses, commissions, administrative fees or overhead from your royalty check.

Regardless of the method of calculating your share of the profits, in many instances, the amount you receive in royalties will vary based on the method of distribution. For example, royalties for sales made via TV spots will generally be lower than retail because of the cost (i.e., buying media spots). Royalties for international sales are generally higher. Again, these are all points for negotiation; an understanding of a licensor's proposed distribution strategy will help you better negotiate royalty percentages.

Many marketers promote your product with a free giveaway - what is commonly referred to as an "upsell" or a "cross promotion." Such offers are intended to entice the buyer to "act now" in order to receive an additional benefit whether for free (i.e., a free oven mitt with the purchase of a pressure cooker) or an additional product at a reduced price at check-out. Either way, upsells or cross-sell techniques can be a great way to significantly improve your sales.

If the marketer does not agree to allow you to share in the profit of a cross-promotion or you don't receive any additional benefit for the free upsell, make sure you are not footing the costs of the shipping and handling! TV offers generally offer a money-back guarantee on their products which allow the buyer to keep the free items. This is another reason why you don't want to allow a distributor to deduct shipping costs as part of the net revenue clause in your contract.

Rule of thumb is that the longer the laundry list of cost

deductions, the less money you will receive. If the distributor or licensor (as the case may be) is intent on offering you a royalty percentage (rather than a fixed dollar amount), make sure you have an attorney review the adjusted gross revenue clause and the allowable deductions to ensure that you are not agreeing to deductions that are overreaching and, in some cases, downright unscrupulous.

SELL-OFF CLAUSES

The termination clause is the provision that typically enables either party to cancel the deal (1) if minimum sales are not met, (2) if either party decides they don't want to continue the business relationship, or (3) because the agreement has expired. Termination clauses also help protect the parties. If one party is not fulfilling their end of the bargain, it gives the "non-breaching" party the ability to get out of the deal.

Greedy's termination clause contained this language (and, most agreements contain a variation of this clause):

> *Upon termination of this Agreement, Greedy may continue to advertise and distribute the product in its inventory or which Greedy had received an order prior to the date of such termination. In each such case, the parties shall continue to perform as though this Agreement was still in effect until each available product has been sold by Greedy.*

On its face, this seems like a reasonable clause, right? Contract ends, orders are in progress, or inventory is on hand, so why not let them fulfill their obligations? WRONG! Here are a few issues with this clause. First, the term is too open-ended. What if Greedy received an order from Target, but a purchase order hadn't yet been issued? Greedy could potentially wait six months to accept the purchase order, thereby dragging out the termination in order to continue advertising your product. Also, the agreement does not prevent them from producing additional units; it simply says it can advertise and distribute the product in its inventory OR fill orders that were received prior to termination.

That is not even the worst part of this clause. Assuming for a moment that the distributor has 100,000 units in its warehouse and wants to make a deal with a liquidator who will take the entire lot for ten cents on the dollar, the next thing you know, you'll see your product on the shelves of the Dollar Store or Big Lots for a mere $9.99, when the product actually retailed for $29.99. The distributor could actually be losing money in this deal or making a mere 25 cents per unit in GROSS profit.

For this reason, Sell-Off clauses should always include: (1) the right of first refusal to buy back your inventory (at a particular price); (2) a minimum Sell-Off price; and (3) a fixed-end term.

If you aren't savvy enough in the negotiation of your termination clause, once you get the rights back to sell your product, it will basically be D.O.A. (that's dead on arrival, folks). You may not be able to sell your product ever again at any price above the bargain basement rate that was advertised at the Dollar Store or on the shelf at Walgreens, let alone attract any other distribution deals. Other terms to address in a termination clause have to do with the operation of websites, Amazon storefronts, etc., and how quickly that will go back under your control. Have a seasoned professional work with you to ensure the proper belts and suspenders are built into your agreements.

MINIMUM GUARANTEES

Greedy also included a standard clause that would grant them the *sole and exclusive right, privilege, and license under any and all rights on a worldwide basis to advertise and distribute the product for a period of one (1) year; renewable for successive one year terms at Greedy's sole discretion.*

However, nothing in that agreement made any reference to minimum sales. This basically means that by signing that agreement, she would lock herself into an exclusive arrangement with a company that has no commitment to sell any particular quantity to maintain that exclusive license on a worldwide basis, year after year. You'd be surprised how many agreements say exactly this. Unless you know to ask for minimum guarantees, the distributor is not going to suggest it either; that goes double for negotiating upfront, non-refundable advances on your royalties - you don't ask; they don't offer.

INTELLECTUAL PROPERTY RIGHTS

Now, for my favorite all-time clause that licensees try to sneak into their agreements:

Greedy at its sole discretion may create and apply for any and all intellectual property rights for the product.

Um...yeah. So, Greedy may decide to file trademarks or patents or copyrights anywhere in the world, and even after the agreement terminates, they will own your intellectual property rights? Why would they want this stuff if they are no longer selling your product unless they plan to continue to sell your product and not pay your royalties? Or maybe, in some alternate universe, you will have to go and license your own intellectual property from THEM!

So, I marked the clause in the agreement as follows:

> Greedy, ~~at its sole discretion~~ may create and apply for any and all intellectual property rights for the product **in the licensee's name. Licensee shall assign the intellectual property rights to Greedy during the Term. The intellectual property rights shall revert back to licensor upon.** ~~Greedy shall be the sole owner of said intellectual property rights, even after the~~ termination of the Term of this Agreement.

There are a number of ways to handle intellectual property clauses, but Greedy's was a great example of what not to do.

INDEMNIFICATION

Indemnification is a matter which an entire chapter could be devoted to because there are many ways to communicate who is responsible for what in the event something goes wrong. Indemnification is a legal term that assigns risk and liability between parties. What you need to know about indemnification clauses is simple: When you enter into a licensing deal, you are claiming that you are the inventor, the product owner, and that you own all the rights and have the ability to enter into a contract with a third party.

Suppose, however, that you are not the actual inventor - maybe your best friend or your neighbor invented it and is going to claim that you stole their idea and they are going to sue you, then what? The licensee just wants to make sure that you did not make any false representations as to your inventorship, and if you did, that they will not be liable if they get sued. The same holds true for the images (if any) or the trademarks (if any) used. They shouldn't be owned by someone else (including your bank in the event you previously filed for bankruptcy and included your patent or trademark as an asset in your disclosures). The licensor also wants to be sure that you didn't already sign another agreement with someone else that would prevent you from entering into an agreement with them. Sounds simple, right? So, why does a typical indemnification clause seem so complicated?

Companies will try to make you responsible (and therefore, liable) for everything that may go wrong - if the product is defective, if the product claims do not support the benefits, if the advertisement pisses off customers, and so on. But consider this, since the company will likely be the one handling the manufacturing, advertising, and making the claims, shouldn't they be the ones to indemnify YOU? Of course, if you are acting as the supplier, then you would need to assume the risks in this regard.

Many people glaze over while reading indemnification clauses; indeed, they can be quite confusing. The simple rule of thumb of indemnity clauses is that you should only take responsibility for things *within your control*. If the distributor is handling the manufacturing and the advertising campaigns, delays in shipping, etc., - it's not your circus, not your monkey - you should not be liable when things go wrong there. And, equally important, you should not be liable for their legal fees to defend any action as it relates to any issues "outside your control," so be sure they didn't sneak that clause in there either!

AUDIT CLAUSE

Audit clauses can make you chuckle. Audits give you

the right to check the books when you believe they have "cooked the books" and did not pay you your fair share. Many limit your ability to look back further than the last quarter; some are more generous and will give you a year. Be sure that you are allowed to conduct annual audits and, if a discrepancy is found, you should be able to look back further. Also, make sure that provision includes a penalty provision (plus the costs of the audit). There's nothing like the threat of a financial penalty to keep people on the up and up.

Lastly, we all know that attorney's fees can be a barrier to enforcing your agreements in the event of a breach or termination. When a legal dispute arises and people take their disputes to court, the basic rule is that each party to a lawsuit must pay its own attorney's fees. However, contractual language may be included in a contract that states that the losing party in a legal dispute has to pay the winning (or "prevailing") side's attorney's fees and costs. An example of that clause is as follows:

> **Attorney's Fees.** *"The prevailing party shall have the right to collect from the other party its reasonable costs and necessary disbursements and attorneys' fees incurred in enforcing this Agreement."*

These are just a few examples of some of the most critical clauses to look for in an agreement, but there are others that are equally important. What is the governing law? Do you go to courts or to arbitration to settle unresolvable disputes? If arbitration, which one - JAMS? AAA? How many arbitrators do you want? These matters are generally dealt with on a case-specific basis, although you should be aware of the serious implications that these provisions have from a cost perspective as well as your overall ability to enforce your agreements.

For my part, when a client presents me with a highly one-sided contract, it speaks volumes of the type of business partner they may be getting into bed with - and companies that try to take advantage of inventors are not ones you want to do get in bed with! Though, understandably, you may have exhausted all other avenues, rather than have anyone jump off the Golden Gate Bridge, it's certainly worth a peek under the sheets to see whether you could negotiate a more favorable deal that is fair for both parties; it just makes for better bedfellows.

FINDING THE TRAP DOOR

Guest Contribution
From Lesia Farmer - Inventor of the Trap Door Colander.

Lesia Farmer, inventor of the *Trap Door Colander*, will excitedly share to anyone willing to listen that, she had some success on the first licensing deal, but for the most part, it was a nightmare because she had the wrong attorneys review her agreement; neither were licensing specialists.

"If you can't do anything else, hire a patent attorney to file the patent for you, and NEVER negotiate a contract without a professional contract attorney! The money you spend, I almost guarantee, you will make back by not signing a half ass agreement!"

I contacted Lesia for an interview. She related that she was still stuck in a licensing agreement that contained auto-renewals but wasn't making any money. After reviewing her agreement and noting that there was a minimum commitment of units to be sold that was not being met, she was able to get out of the deal and put her product in front of other possible distributors. Lesia is now in the process of finalizing a new distribution deal for her product.

TOP TAKEAWAYS

- *Agreements are negotiable.*

- *You have better leverage when you're operating from a position of strength.*

- *It's wise to hire an attorney to negotiate your deals than to have to hire one to get you out of a deal. You'll save time, money and aggravation.*

"...In the event of a Zombie Appocalpse we own the rights for the 'DieMonde-Sword' and at our sole discretion may create and apply for any and all intellectual property rights for the product."

5 A PATENT INJUSTICE

We think we have solved the mystery of creation. Maybe we should patent the universe and charge everyone royalties for their existence. - Stephen Hawking

The problem with patents is not whether you can get them; it's whether you can enforce them. Patent litigation is expensive. It means that bigger corporations (frequently backed by their insurers), who have deeper pockets and a team of lawyers, will drain an inventor's resources even before they have had their day in court. Patent ownership is like owning an expensive foreign car; it's a great pleasure when it's working, but when something goes wrong, it's expensive to fix.

There are certain things in life we'd like to do but may not be able to afford. My daughter's friend got hooked on horseback riding when she was young. As she progressed in her skills and her passion for competition grew, so did the price tag for her parents. What started off as a few lessons a month for roughly $300.00 progressed to a $15,000 + a year expense for boarding a horse, trainers, competitions, and the costs of travel. Had her parents been unable to afford that hefty price tag, her dreams of one day becoming an equestrian would never have come to fruition – instead, she may have been persuaded to join a soccer team or engage in another less costly pastime. Similarly, if you don't have enough money to hire a patent attorney, you shouldn't be an inventor, as getting a patent is the cheapest part of getting your product to market. I'm not saying that all products need to be patented and, in some instances, copyrights and trademark protection will be sufficient. Though, many inventors fail to factor in intellectual property in their budgets.

I consult with new inventors on a weekly basis. Understandably, one of the first questions that they have is how much it will cost to file a patent. For those who are unfamiliar or only have a general idea of what a patent does, a patent is a set of exclusive rights granted by government to an inventor or an assignee for a limited period of time in exchange for publicly disclosing the invention. A patent application consists of a set of specifications (describing your product), drawings, and one or more claims that describes the usefulness, uniqueness, and novelty of your invention.

In order to get a clear picture of the range in costs, it is helpful to understand the various patents that can be applied for. Utility patents, which have a lifespan of 20 years, protect the functional aspects of an invention, and design patents, which have a lifespan of 15 years, protect the appearance (i.e. ornamental design). As the cost of filing a utility or design patent (also known as a non-provisional patent or NPA) is high, oftentimes, an inventor decides to file a Provisional Patent Application (PPA), which is essentially a shortened version of your patent application. A PPA grants you one year to seek possible licensing deals without losing your rights to your idea.

The benefits of a PPA is that it is a fraction of the cost of other patent filings, which means you can test out the waters to see if you get any bites while, at the same time, preserving your rights to file a utility patent application. Otherwise, if you try to sell a product to the public that isn't patented at the time you market it, you will lose your rights to filing a patent. One year after filing your provisional patent, you must file a utility patent or the rights to your invention will be forfeited forever.

Determining what type of patent is most suitable depends on (1) what element(s) of your creation is/are novel and (2) your budget. It is a business decision that has to be made with careful consideration.

While the cost can range anywhere from $3500-$5000 for a provisional patent (that protects you temporarily while you try to market your invention) and between $10,000-18,000 (depending on the complexity) for a full-blown utility patent (aka a non-provisional patent), patenting is just one of the costs of getting started as an inventor.

Engineering and costs of molds could run you up to $75,000 not to mention legal fees, marketing costs (branding, logo, packaging, website development, infomercial, just to name a few line items) and let's not forget, cost of inventory.

I'm not trying to scare you off here. It's important to consider this - a patent is either a business or a business opportunity. Are you looking to build a business around your idea or license your idea? If it's a business, pure and simple, it's risky and capital-intensive. In addition to paying for the costs of developing, patenting, and prototyping, you will need marketing, advertising, manufacturing, billing fulfillment, and distribution – maybe even staff and office space. If it's a business opportunity, then you are looking at a licensing model. Either way, there are costs involved and the cost of a patent is part of the cost of doing business. Patent lawyers are known to say, "A patent is worth nothing or it's worth a lot." Do you have $20,000 to spend to explore your business opportunity? If not, you just talked yourself out of a patent!

To Patent or Not to Patent?

Many licensees prefer to license a patented product because it gives them greater comfort (though, not a guarantee) that no one else will be able to market the same product. Also, if someone does infringe on your patent, you have the right to bring an infringement action.

Simply stated, if you have a product that has multiple years of shelf life, you'll need a patent. However, if you have a product that has a short-term life span, or is seasonal, a provisional patent enables you to quickly get in and get out at a reduced financial risk.

A few things to remember is that *Snuggies*® (basically a blanket with arm-holes) was never patented, but, it was one of those products that sold millions. Many may not remember similar products on the market named the *Snuggly*® and *Slanket*®, and several other knock-off brands, but because *Snuggie*® jumped out there first to market, made a name, and sold, sold, sold; they were lucky. This is not something that normally happens with every product that isn't patented, but it does go to show that products can make millions without a valid patent.

You may have noticed that some everyday products are marked "patent pending," "patent applied for," or "patent application serial number 123345678"; however, what do these terms actually mean, and what purpose do they serve? For the most part, the only purpose served is to put others on notice that a patent has been applied for and hopefully, to deter others from copying your invention. Now, here is the kicker...when a patent is pending, it has not yet acquired any rights that enable the inventor to exclude others from making or selling that product. In other words, while a patent is pending, you don't have any enforceable rights.

Randy Cooper, the inventor of the *Noodlehead Sprinkler*, learned all too well that his "patent pending" registration did nothing to stave off the copycat products that emerged from his innovation and eventually eroded all his profits. Randy was a mechanical design engineer for 35 years. As an avid gardener, who lived on a steeply sloped property, Randy had trouble finding a sprinkler that could get the job done. They all appeared to have shortcomings. After watching his wife put "Benders" in her hair each night, Randy had the "Eureka" moment for solving his watering problems -- to create a lawn and garden sprinkler with bendable tubes -- and started to develop prototypes. After years of development and refinement, the *Noodlehead Sprinkler* was born!

However, while Randy's patent was still pending (it can take up to 2-3 years to actually receive a patent registration), numerous copycats popped up; most notably the *Spyder Sprinkler*. This device was virtually visually identical, however of inferior quality to Randy's invention (except that it sold at a lower price) and under a different name. Randy and his wife, Marlene Dumas, were naturally devastated... who is going to buy the more expensive version of the same product? Eventually, the bulk of Randy's sales dwindled away. Randy and Marlene began to fight against the infringers, but what recourse did they have? There were no patent rights to defend, since no patent had yet been granted by the USPTO. Nonetheless, the couple fought tooth and nail by sending cease and desist notices. Sadly, Randy passed away on March 29, 2015. Grief-stricken by the loss of her husband and the belief that his battle with the copycats weakened his resolve to fight the battle with his health, Marlene has not yet pursued the matter further.

Josh Malone, inventor of *Bunch 0 Balloons*, (a toy gadget that blows up 100 water balloons in under one minute using a special hose attachment that affixes to a garden hose), is quoted as saying that his patent has cost him $17M and could end up costing him $50M. A year after his successful Kickstarter campaign (raising approximately $930,000), his product was knocked off by Telebrands and Walmart (selling under names such as *Balloon Bonanza*, *Battle Balloons*, and *Easy Einstein Balloons*). Rather than concede infringement, Telebrands fought to invalidate Malone's patents ever since. The dispute highlights how the launch of a successful new product is frequently followed by the arrival of copycat products, which can trigger expensive patent disputes and invalidation proceedings. Josh is fortunate that the company who has licensed his product backed the lawsuit through the multiple attacks waged by Telebrands. Josh's harrowing experience will forever be known as the most expensive water balloon fight of the century.

Let's Do this!! Where should I file my patent?

If you are a U.S. based inventor, the United States Patent and Trademark office is the place you'd file. However, what many people don't consider is the need (and the costs) to patent your invention where you manufacture or sell your product -- particularly in the top counterfeit countries. For example, if you are manufacturing in China and don't have a patent filed there, there is nothing to stop someone from filing YOUR patent in China. (See Chapter 8 -If you Lie Down with Dogs You Will Get Fleas, which discusses how the manufacturer of the Woof Washer 360 did just that!) China (like most countries), operates on a first-to-file system. More importantly, no one is actually reviewing utility patents filed in China to be sure they haven't been filed elsewhere first (in other words, China is a self-policing patent filing system). This means that anyone (including your manufacturer) can file a patent application in China and receive a patent, and you may not even know it until after it has been issued! Therefore, it is up to the individual or company to then challenge the patent in, what is called an invalidation proceeding. These proceedings can take years (not to mention thousands or even millions of dollars) before a decision is rendered. In the meantime, the infringer can continue to sell your product - most often, at a lower cost than your own product, thus, depriving you of thousands (or millions) of dollars in revenues that you may never recoup.

Not surprisingly, most counterfeits originate from mainland China. This is due in part to the fact that China is the largest manufacturer of so many products — most of which are made cheaply. Amazon makes it very easy for China to sell products to U.S. consumers, and preferred shipping rates offered through the U.S. Postal Service, makes it cheaper for Chinese sellers to ship goods direct to the consumer, than for sellers shipping within the U.S.

If you have no direct relationship with your manufacturer (perhaps you found them through Alibaba or a third party), you have no idea whether that company is producing counterfeit goods). Adding to that list - Singapore, Hong Kong, India, and Taiwan are also included in the top five countries where counterfeits are produced. The top items that are knocked off often include handbags and wallets, apparel, consumer electronics, watches, jewelries, and toys.

The Netherlands is surprisingly high on the list for distributing counterfeit goods. If you are on a tight budget and it was already a hardship to file your patent in the U.S., at a minimum, my advice to you is that a patent should be filed *any-*

where your product may be manufactured or sold. In many cases, your lawyer may be able to negotiate with your distributor to bear the international patenting and renewal costs (provided they name you as the inventor) as a condition to you granting them exclusive rights to distribute your product during the term of your agreement.

By now you should have a clear picture: Nothing about inventing is cheap, and without money or at least darn good intellectual property rights, chances of success are pretty slim. Now, it is up to you to decide just "how beautiful your baby is."

Does the product have global appeal or is it marketable only in the US? If global, an international patent and trademark strategy is essential.

Sounds costly? Don't be discouraged, many inventors launch products on a shoestring budget provided they have the right guidance and possibly even backing from a distributor to flip the bill when it comes to future patent or trademark filings, renewals and enforcement.

Danielle Strachman, Founder and General Partner at 1517 Fund (1517fund.com), an early stage investment company that invests in projects that are led by young founders has this to say about patents:

> We work with very green entrepreneurs who often have an inventor's mindset. It is our belief that at the earliest stages, before a Series A funding round, companies often are not "rich enough for justice" to fight patent infringement. That said, where we think patents serve a big purpose is defining property rights for licensing, new fund raising rounds, and potential acquisitions. So, it's definitely important to think about the process and defining IP, for us it's just a question of when.

US005826803A

United States Patent [19]

Cooper

[11] **Patent Number:** **5,826,803**

[45] **Date of Patent:** **Oct. 27, 1998**

[54] **LAWN AND GARDEN SPRINKLER WITH BENDABLE TUBES**

[76] Inventor: **Randy J. Cooper**, 12273 Circula Panorama, Santa Ana, Calif. 92705

[21] Appl. No.: **854,524**

[22] Filed: **May 12, 1997**

Related U.S. Application Data

[63] Continuation of Ser. No. 394,716, Feb. 27, 1995, abandoned.

[51] Int. Cl.⁶ **B05B 1/14**
[52] U.S. Cl. **239/556**
[58] Field of Search .... 239/548, 556, 239/562, 588, 553.1, 590.3, DIG. 1, DIG. 12

[56] **References Cited**

U.S. PATENT DOCUMENTS

400,683	4/1889	Jackson	239/548 X
1,484,575	2/1924	Shulin	239/588 X
1,989,525	1/1935	Moore	239/588 X
2,757,960	8/1956	Hatcher	239/229
2,968,443	1/1961	Manning	239/562 X
3,301,490	1/1967	Hruby, Jr.	239/548 X
3,402,741	9/1968	Yurdin	239/588 X
5,312,047	5/1994	Akers	239/562 X

Primary Examiner—Robert J. Oberleitner
Assistant Examiner—C. T. Bartz
Attorney, Agent, or Firm—Edgar W. Averill, Jr.

[57] **ABSTRACT**

A lawn and garden sprinkler which has a manifold with one or more bendable tubes extending therefrom. The tubes can be bent to direct one or more streams of water to a desired location. In a preferred design, there is an internal water flow restrictor which permits a larger flow of water from some tubes than others so that a maximum control of water dispersion is obtained. Also in a preferred configuration, the bendable tubes are made from a flexible material and have a ductile wire within them.

13 Claims, 3 Drawing Sheets

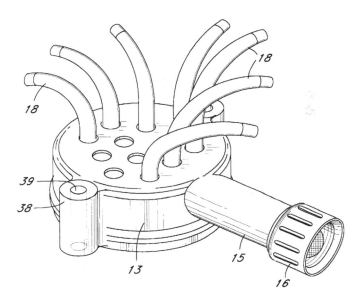

Randy Cooper's *Noodlehead Sprinkler* **- U.S. Patent 5,826,803 -**

"I invented the 'Snoog-E' ~ I am therefore the lawful owner of the patent."

6

COPYRIGHTS: THE SCRAPPY INVENTOR'S BEST FRIEND

The way to wealth is as plain as the way to market. It depends chiefly on two words, industry and frugality: that is, waste neither time nor money, but make the best use of both. Without industry and frugality nothing will do, and with them everything. - **Benjamin Franklin**

It's a bird...it's a plane...it's a federally registered copyright? That's right, folks, the copyright has been spotted in numerous counterfeit and infringement lawsuits saving product owners significant losses by activating statutory (automatic and guaranteed) damages. While patents and trademarks get all of the publicity for protecting brands and products, the copyright fights infringement more effectively than its intellectual property (IP) counterparts, making it the unsung hero of IP protection.[1]

A copyright grants the creator the exclusive right to use, make copy, license, and otherwise exploit a literary, musical, or artistic work, whether printed, audio, music, video, etc. Works created on or after January 1, 1978, are protected for

---

1   Reprinted with permission; Digital Law Group blog (2018) (co-authors Paula Brillson Phillips & Jessica Sutherland).

the lifetime of the author or creator plus 70 years after his or her death. The rights that exist for 70 years following the death of the creator enables the creator's family (or beneficiaries) to continue to profit from the works that were created by their loved ones, carry on the family business or otherwise enjoy the fruits of their labors (through the receipt of royalties, for example).

The copyright is so overlooked that even product attorneys forget what a powerful member of the IP protection league it is. For example, patent rights enforcement is technical and complex and often requires long, costly legal battles with Tony Stark caliber experts to prove infringement. However, copyrights, which protect property such as images, illustrations, infomercials, and product packaging, are pretty easy to eyeball, even for an untrained juror.

Copyright is also the most affordable IP protection to secure (e.g., $35 per image to register and $55 to register up to 750 images). Moreover, copyright infringement triggers statutory damages that can soar up to $30,000 per occurrence; plus, recovery of attorney's fees if you file your copyright within 90 days of using it. As such, trial attorneys are more willing to take on a (properly registered) copyright infringement case on a contingency basis, which means you won't have to pay anything upfront. Of course, statutory damages are merely a fallback, with many product owners wanting to recover actual damages (i.e., lost profits), which is an entirely different hulk of a task.

Additionally, the copyright is the only member of the IP protection league that successfully combats counterfeit sales on platforms such as Amazon; trademark registration alone will not suffice to remove counterfeits on Amazon. To be sure, the counterfeit seller merely has to allege that it is selling a legitimate product, and then there is no infringement thanks to the *First Sale Doctrine* (This provides that an individual who purchases a copy of a copyrighted work owns the title to it. He or she can sell, display or otherwise dispose of *that particular copy*, without violating the rights of the copyright owner). Counterfeiters tend to overlook this salient point when they use original images to promote products online.

In some instances, the infringer changes the name of the product, which effectively shields it from a trademark infringement claim altogether. However, the right to resell a product does not give rise to the right to display *copyrighted images* for the purpose of that sale. This is another reason why the copyright is so powerful.

Most product marketers and distributors have likely had to deal with counterfeit products being sold on e-commerce platforms such as Amazon and eBay, among others. Although some counterfeit goods and knockoffs are obviously fake, others use the original product's copyrighted images and trademarks, making it hard for consumers to distinguish a fake from the original. As a result, the product owner can suffer serious economic harm, as many consumers turn to these sites to purchase products. The good news is, most of them, including Amazon and eBay, have systems in place for reporting and subsequently removing infringing listings. The bad news is, these systems are somewhat ineffective for permanently removing serious, repeat infringers.

When dealing with infringement on Amazon and eBay, the process usually goes something like this: You search for your product on the platform and find an unauthorized listing (or oftentimes, several) that displays your trademark and images from your product website. You (or your attorney) fill out the infringement report provided by the platform, and typically within 48 hours, you receive the notice that a reported listing has been removed. Unfortunately, in many instances, the listing goes right back up because the seller is not prohibited from relisting a product after being reported and removed for infringement. Thus, takedowns become a frustrating game of whack-a-mole (you know the arcade game where players use a mallet to hit randomly appearing toy moles back into their holes) until it ultimately becomes apparent that the infringer is not giving up.

In these situations, copyrights become the product owner's greatest intellectual property asset. It is important to note that copyright does not protect the mechanical or utilitarian aspects of a product. It may, however, protect any graphic, pictorial, or sculptural authorship that can be identified separately from the useful aspects of an object. For example, a pillow design (such as a ruffle) could be protected by copyright but, the pillow itself could not.

See https://www.copyright.gov/circs/circ40.pdf.

If an infringer is using images, videos, or text from the product website or infomercial, you can request a subpoena from the clerk of any United States district court for the identification of the infringer, without filing a civil action. Although this may seem like a tedious process, it can be much more efficient than continuously reporting the same infringers.

For Example: A Hat Design (such as lens/film & gelpack) could be protected by a copyright but, the hat itself could not.

> Copyright is a law that gives you ownership over the things you create. Whether it be an illustration (drawing) of your product that you include in your patent application or on your website or business plans, a photograph, text on your website, music, or packaging, it's the copyright law itself that assures that ownership. The ownership of that copyright comes with several rights that you, as the owner, have exclusively. Those rights include:
>
> - **The right to publicly display (or perform - as in music or dance moves) your works (websites, product packaging, and commercials);**
>
> - **to prepare derivative works;**
>
> - **to distribute or disseminate copies;**
>
> - **to perform the work (i.e., air infomercials or demonstrations).**

I am such a strong believer in the value of copyrights that I taught my son, Julien, who is a composer and musician, how to file copyrights for his musical scores when he was just 12 years old.

Many clients ask whether mailing themselves a letter containing their copyrighted materials is sufficient to show that they are the owner of the materials. While this may be useful to show first use, posting on the Internet is just as effective in publishing your works. However, neither of these methods is sufficient to enforce your copyrights. You will have to officially register your works if you wish to bring a lawsuit for infringement of a U.S. published work.

Works "made for hire" are an important exception to the general rule for claiming copyright. For example, if you hired (and paid) a web developer or a graphic artist, a product designer, or a photographer or videographer to help you, it would make sense that the person who hired (and paid) that third party should be considered the owner of the work, right?

Whether a work is made for hire is determined by the facts that exist at the time the work is created. There are two situations in which a work may be made for hire:

- **When the work is created by an employee as part of the employee's regular duties, or**

- **When an individual and the hiring party enter into a written agreement that the work is to be considered a "work made for hire" and the work is specially ordered or commissioned.**

A photographer took photos for a client's website (we'll call her Justis Santiago). The agreement was that Santiago would only pay for the images that she chose. Subsequently, the photographer uploaded over 100 images to her website and Santiago chose three. A year later, Santiago noticed that the photographer prominently displayed on her website those images that Santiago did not select, and therefore, didn't pay for. The photographer argued that she owned the rights to these images because Santiago did not pay her for them.

In this kind of arrangement, you can see how a dispute could easily arise if the Work for Hire agreement was silent with respect to the images that Santiago did not pay for (or, if you didn't have an agreement in place at all - which is also fairly common). That is why it is important to have a clear understanding, in writing - whether it be unused footage or unused drafts of product design - to avoid legal disputes. After sending several cease and desist notices to the photographer, she eventually relented and removed the images. But, what if she had refused? Ms. Santiago would have been faced with a decision to either sue the photographer in court or forego her rights to the images.

In October 2013, Milo & Gabby sued Amazon for trademark infringement and copyright infringement, among other claims. Milo & Gabby is a small family business that designs and sells "animal-shaped" pillowcases. It discovered that knock-offs were listed for sale on Amazon's website. The images used to promote these products contained images that were taken from the copyright owner's own webpage and Amazon listings. The products were actually offered for sale by third party sellers, and all but one did their own fulfillment. One of the merchants used Amazon's fulfillment service, but that was not sufficient for the courts to hold Amazon liable. In fact, multiple infringement cases that have been filed against Amazon have all been dismissed on the basis Amazon is immune under the Digital Millennium Copyright Act (DMCA) which protects service providers/platforms, such as Amazon, from infringement claims. Other platforms, such as Kickstarter are also escaping liability from the way the current laws are drafted. There is no doubt that we now live in a time where the law lags behind technology and new legislation is needed to hold service providers liable for enabling infringing activities.

Intellectual property is only as strong as the money you are willing to spend on enforcement. You cannot rely on platforms like Kickstarter, Facebook, and Amazon to help you, unless you pay for an attorney to send them complaint letters directly. Shopify is the best/fastest to respond and take action, as long as they can see that your copyrighted images are being used, and/or trademarks are being violated. If the knockoff art-ists get creative, they will start taking your images, and there-fore, makes them harder to enforce unless you have registered your copyrights.

In 2018, impulse-buying millennials spent approxi-mately $482 million on counterfeit products on Black Friday. This year, the trend is set to continue, as it is predicted that one-in-four will purchase counterfeit items due to the buyer's inability to spot counterfeiters and the marketplace's attitude toward counterfeit sellers online. Considering that this year's online holiday spending is predicted to exceed $124 billion from November – December (with over $23 billion from Thanksgiving to Cyber Monday alone!), it is imperative that buyers beware, and that product marketers actively police their online listings, lest their sales and reputations get gob-bled up by counterfeiters.

Additionally, last year, nearly a quarter of counterfeits purchased by millennials were done via social media sites such as Facebook and Instagram; thus, monitoring these platforms is essential to brand protection and a successful holiday shop-ping season.

Whether you are a shopper or a seller, here are some keys to identifying counterfeits online:

- Deep discounts. A deal that is too good to be true is likely just that. If you can purchase a big brand product like MAC lipstick or BEATS by DRE at a very big discount, the product is likely a fake one.

- Shipping from China. Products shipped directly from China can be a red flag, as most (not all) legitimate U.S. products are shipped from U.S. distribution/fulfillment centers.

- Unverified third-party sellers. Most reputable online sellers also have their own product websites (e.g., snuggiestore.com). Do a web search prior to purchase to find out whether the seller is the same as the one listed on Amazon, and whether there is a major price difference in the products.

- Typically, you won't know if you purchased a fake product until you have received your shipment. Signs to look out for are:
  >Packaging that is flimsy or has misspelled words.
  >No country of origin or manufacturer contact information on either the packaging or the product itself.
  >Electronics that do not have the UL (Underwriters Laboratory Label). This is particularly concerning, as counterfeit electronics can be a safety hazard.

Policing the sale of goods online can be a daunting and time-consuming task for product marketers — especially if a product is being heavily counterfeited. It also doesn't help that each marketplace has a different system (some more user-friendly than others) for reporting and ultimately removing counterfeit goods and storefronts.

While patents and trademarks are formidable tools for many reasons other than defending against knockoffs and counterfeits, with the copyright being such a low-cost titan in the IP universe, it's surprising that more businesses do not utilize its protection. For maximum protection, copyrights need to be registered as soon as possible, so be sure to summon an intellectual property attorney prior to your product rollout.

7   JUST GOOGLE® IT!

You need to turn over every rock and open every door to learn your industry. This process never ends. - **Mark Cuban**

Going into business with someone, hiring a consultant, a supplier (or even a lawyer or accountant) is a huge commitment and could have serious negative repercussions if the person (or company) turns out to be less than scrupulous. Performing personal due diligence (not to be confused with corporate due diligence) does not necessarily mean ordering a credit or criminal background check in the manner that many employers do, or doing a deep dive into their corporate or financial records. It may mean something as simple as just Googling it to see if there are any negative reports about a person or a business.

There is a wealth of information available to you at your fingertips. Type in a person's name, company or product name and you can perform a cursory search of anyone and anything. Yet, you'd be surprised how few people avail themselves of this easily accessible, vast resource when it comes to choosing business partners or vendors. By using publicly available information (as outlined below), you can check out your potential partner to determine whether they are an upstanding match for you.

The number one fear inventors face is that someone is going to steal their ideas. Everyone is afraid that if you show your idea to a company, they will knock you off. However, many companies that specialize in getting products to the market and moving products into the tentacles of our supply chains don't necessarily specialize in innovation and therefore, are happy to partner with someone who does.

When you go out and submit your idea, the truth is, *you don't know if they are going to knock you off and steal your idea*, so you have to make sure you are dealing with reputable folks. To this end, don't simply upload your business idea to any website that advertises that they can make you as rich as George Foreman, don't provide anyone with a copy of your patent or even patent #, and certainly don't pay anyone money who says they will market your product and get you a distribution deal UNLESS YOU'VE DONE YOUR RESEARCH! You can't do market research/competitive analysis too early.

> *>TACTICS, TIPS & MORE >> PAGES 131 - 133*
> *To learn some insights into a typical investigation process.*

There are also those review sites, such as RipOffReport. com, that we don't personally trust. They offer a service to remove the negative reports under their so-called Corporate Advocacy Program. Xcentric Ventures, RipOffReport's parent company has been sued by multiple companies throughout the United States, accused of extortion (by asking for money in exchange for removing negative reviews). However, courts have held that RipOffReport is merely a platform and does not control the content posted on its site. As such, while there are still numerous pending lawsuits against them for libel, defamation, and extortion pending, so far they have been successful in warding off liability. In short, whenever a negative report is removed from RipoffReport or Consumer Reports, be skeptical as to why that report was removed.

No, it doesn't take a rocket scientist (or a lawyer) to understand the importance of conducting due diligence on an individual or company before signing agreements or entering into business relationships. It may, however, make sense to contact a lawyer to assist in your due diligence process — which could cost anywhere from $250 to $1000 depending on the size and scope of the investigation.

GOOGLE® YOURSELF

Dawn Sole, Miami entrepreneur and inventor of the *Pluck N' File* (a "Swiss Army knife of Beauty Tools" that includes a tweezer, an eyebrow comb, a nail file and a buffer), learned that someone stole her business idea by simply Googling her company's name. Her patented, trademarked product, was ready to go to market after having signed an agreement with a large manufacturer - all she needed was the capital to pay for tooling and purchase inventory. Dawn decided to raise money online using a crowdfunding site.

While the concept of crowdfunding has been around for centuries, it is still formally recognized as a new industry with the passage of the Jumpstart Our Business Startups Act ("JOBS Act") in 2012 allowing for the "funding a project or venture by raising many small amounts of money from a large number of people, typically via the Internet." There are numerous donation crowdfunding platforms where entrepreneurs can ask for capital such as Kickstarter, Indiegogo, GoFundMe, RocketHub, or Fundly. Some sites cater to strictly non-profit endeavors, while others are more artistic or entrepreneurial in nature. According to Massolution's Crowdfunding Industry 2015 report, over $34 Billion was raised in 2015 alone and, no doubt, that amount has dramatically increased in the 4 years since this report was published.

Sole created an Indiegogo crowdfunding campaign in November 2014 after Kickstarter rejected her "personal care project" as it did not fit into one of their existing funding categories (which at the time were limited to technology projects).

After the Indiegogo campaign launched, Sole was surprised and disheartened by the lackluster response - she was short of achieving her goal of $25,000. Her instincts told her something was wrong, so she decided to Google her own company's name, and BAM! she found that someone had created a *mirror* funding site of her Indiegogo campaign on Kickstarter! The campaign images and descriptions were copied word for word from her Indiegogo site and had raised about $27,000. Her own campaign had raised less.

A cease-and-desist letter was sent to Kickstarter and they subsequently suspended the fundraising campaign and froze the funds. While that was a small victory for Sole, she was concerned that the confusion that this "suspension" caused could damage her reputation since Kickstarter refused to completely remove the listing from their site. "When people see it on Kickstarter, they're going to see *Pluck N' File* and they're going to assume that it's me," she said. "They're going to think, why was it suspended? What did *Pluck N' File* do wrong?"

She obviously wishes that Kickstarter would simply remove the campaign, but according to their policies, once suspended, it will be suspended permanently. Still now, the webpage where the fraudulent campaign was listed states that the project "is the subject of an intellectual property dispute and is currently unavailable." Kickstarter also refused to provide the identity of the fraudulent lister (or pay her any of the funds the trickster raised - those backers will be entitled to refunds). Although she would have been able to subpoena such information, Sole decided to put the matter on the back burner while she focused on the continued roll-out of her product. However, the person behind the fake Kickstarter campaign may eventually face liabilities for intellectual property infringement and unfair competition.

Sole's Indiegogo campaign closed on January 2, 2018 though, she was able to raise enough funds to get her project off the ground. She is still seeking a lucrative distribution deal, but through this experience she has learned to be on the lookout for fraud or anyone else who tries to ride the coattails of her products. She wishes that Kickstarter would close down the fake campaign or at least redirect donors to her real page on Indiegogo — but until then, the *Pluck N' File* creator will fight the company tooth and nail.

The most important lesson Dawn wants to share with this world, knowing that "this has definitely happened to other people because I could see the loopholes," is, she says, "If I could make a difference with my story, I have no problem being the example of what could happen if you're not careful and you're not doing your homework."

Internationally, there are a host of other scams you should be aware of. When you file a trademark, patent, or copyright with the USPTO or other IP-related government entity, your application becomes public information. So-called marketing companies (scammers), many located outside of the U.S., take this information to solicit you for unnecessary services that seem to be related to your intellectual property. There are number of these deceptive marketing practices that some of you may fall prey to if you are not aware that they are actually scams.

The solicitations may include:

- *Offers for legal services to file your IP in another country.*

- *Trademark monitoring services.*

- *Invoices for renewals (coinciding with your registration dates).*

- *Recordation fees for trademark registration.*

- *Offers to include your trademark listing on private registries or directories.*

- *Invoices for foreign registration.*

While most of us are pretty cognizant of online scams, even the best of us can be duped by these guys; however, there are some basic things you should do to ensure you do not fall victim to a scam:

- *Check the source of the official correspondence - communication from the USPTO comes from an address in Alexandria, Virginia or an email return address that ends in "@uspto. gov."*

- *Research the name of the organization that sent out the invoice and see whether they show up on any watch lists.*

- *Read the document. If it is a "legal" trick, it will say somewhere (even in very small print) that it's a solicitation, not an official invoice. You will probably note bad grammar and misspelled words in the solicitation as well.*

- *Work with your lawyer or other providers to help verify the authenticity and accuracy of any invoice before paying it.*

"I'm not sure I trust these *Humans* enough to do business with them. I mean, have you seen the mess they've made of their planet? We'll have to do some more research."

KEY TAKEAWAYS

- **Learning about the potential market position of your invention is critical to commercialization success. For more information about market positioning, reference:** Ries A. Trout J. Positioning: The Battle for Your Mind. McGraw-Hill Education, 2001.

- **Understanding what information to collect, from whom, and selecting the more effective ways of acquiring it will support you in making informed decisions. To access printable forms and reference some of the many tools you can use for interviewing key executives, reference the Workbook** in the Appendix of Docie R. The Inventor's Bible: How to Market and License Your Brilliant Ideas. Penguin/Random House, 2015.

- **You can perform market research and prepare a competitive analysis at any stage of product development, even before patenting, and potentially without the need for disclosure agreements.**

- **You can't do market research/competitive analysis too early, but you can do it too late.**

- **Direct contact with people, either in-person or at least verbally, helps facilitate both success with research, and may lead to the building of relationships that results in concluding successful business arrangements.**

8

IF YOU LIE DOWN WITH DOGS YOU GET FLEAS

All that was great in the past was ridiculed, condemned, combated, suppressed--only to emerge all the more powerfully, all the more triumphantly from the struggle.
- Nikola Tesla

Ryan Diez conceived of the *Woof Washer 360*® back in 1994 when, as a child, he and his dad had difficulty washing their Labrador Retriever. He encountered all of the challenges any given person could expect to face when inventing a product, scrapping one prototype after the next as he learned and honed his skills at inventing.

Enter *Woof Washer 360* – designed as a hoop with water spouts and a shampoo container that is attached to a hose or other water source and voila! – no more need to touch that dirty dog!

According to various sources, he promised his dad that one day, his product would be on the shelves. Ryan filed his patent, obtained a distribution agreement with New York based Matthew Ackerman (of R and H Direct, Inc.) and he believed that he was on the road to doggone riches.

The product launched in June 2015, using an infomercial that was so brilliantly produced, R and H Direct signed Marketing Maven to handle the public relations and social media marketing. After Marketing Maven obtained an edited version of the animation portion of the video without text, without voiceover, and without the offer, they seeded it internationally and it turned into a viral sensation, garnering nearly 68 million views. It received 143,000 comments and was shared over 1.1 million times. That weekend, Marketing Maven social media executive's email was overloaded with over 4,000 direct messages from *Woof Washer 360*'s Facebook account. Many of these messages were from international distributors looking to carry the product or from consumers asking if they could receive it in a specific country.

Shortly thereafter, Marketing Maven received requests from *The TODAY show* and *Good Morning America* producers both asking for an exclusive segment. No exclusivity was given, so both national morning broadcast shows aired segments, along with *CNET* and *The Weather Channel*. The launch campaign won awards through the Public Relations Society of America (PRSA) at their annual PRISM Awards, as well as finalist in the North American Excellence Awards. You can see the award-winning video at www.woofwasher360.com.

Victims of their success?

Amidst the great media buzz, R and H was naturally anxious to start taking customer orders. However, when the product samples were received, they had a myriad of problems - the streams of water shot out in multiple directions instead of directly towards the center of the hoop, causing the user to become soaked. The product also lacked any water pressure, as though there was a water restrictor on the handle and, the labels were blurry and affixed upside down. These issues were still unresolved when it came time to demonstrate the *Woof Washer 360* on live television in the press segments. Marketing Maven had to make sure the spokesperson had functional equipment (and a well-behaved dog) to showcase the product in the best light. It was a very stressful time.

As they eagerly awaited shipment of the new samples and became anxious that they were not going to meet the deadline to ship to customers who had already purchased the product, suddenly, bad reviews of the product began cropping up everywhere. They were seriously baffled, as no units had been shipped.

To everyone's surprise, our quick Google searches pulled up multiple listings for the *Woof Washer 360* on Amazon, eBay and Alibaba, just less than one month after the video went viral. No one could understand how there was already a third-party seller! The attorneys began to diligently report infringing listings on Amazon, eBay, and Alibaba, but as fast as the listings came down, new ones came up - it was like playing whack-a-mole. The Chinese manufacturer was contacted but seemed to have no knowledge of how this could have possibly happened. However, these bootleg units weren't just similar, *they were identical right down to the blurry upside-down logos!* This surely was not coincidental. Even, more troubling, the Amazon listing was using all of the pictures and screenshots from the commercial that had gone viral – a blatant theft of intellectual property. How could anyone expect the product to sell on TV when the fraudulent listings on Amazon were selling for cheaper and with free shipping?

Amazon.com is a market leader and is often the first place consumers go for hassle-free and instant purchases. This was a major concern and the worst nightmare for a product which was just launching.

While everyone involved continued to battle with the manufacturer, they were completely blindsided when they learned that the manufacturer filed trademark and patent applications for Ryan's intellectual property in China, naming themselves as the inventor! They didn't invent anything. The manufacturer simply beat Ryan to the punch in filing the China patent - since China (like most countries) is a first-to-file system; even if an inventor has a patent in the U.S. or elsewhere, these inventions are not protected in China unless you file a patent there as well. In a first-to-file system, the right to the grant of a patent for a given invention lies with the first person to file a patent application for protection of that invention, regardless of the date of actual invention. It is for this reason that, as previously stated, clients are advised to file a patent in the country they intend to manufacture (which, most often, is China) *prior* to the start of manufacture.

Due to the overwhelming consumer demand for the viral success of *Woof Washer 360*, R and H Direct landed a large distribution deal with Telebrands and they undertook to redesign the product. The new version of the product was a true example of quality manufacturing, and has been extremely well-received, according to Ackerman. So well, in fact, that the largest big box retailers, including, but not limited to Target, Walmart, and PetSmart, all stocked it. TV shopping channels such as *Home Shopping Network* and *Evine* (formerly *Shop NBC*) both featured the product on live segments. But, sadly, the damage to the *Woof Washer 360* brand was done and these units simply sat on the retailers' shelves; they were poorly received. It took over 18 months to retrieve the intellectual property rights in China and finally, success was achieved after spending thousands of dollars (as China law governs intellectual property rights, it was necessary to hire local counsel there).

One doesn't normally think of his or her own manufacturer as its toughest competitor. The sad truth of the matter is that many fakes on the market are produced by the inventor's own factory and while this fact was never confirmed, it was highly suspected. A factory could make copies of your molds, for instance, and sell them to a sister factory, they may be selling off the surplus they have, or make a modified version of your product (i.e., change the color or, some other minor aspect). If your only protection was a contract governed by the laws of the U.S., your contract may not even be enforceable in China, or if it is, you may be looking at hefty legal bills to bring your action there; a prospect that many small inventors can't fathom.

Ryan, like many inventors, has become somewhat of a statistic of those being taken advantage of by overseas companies. He has never given up and the well-crafted, redesigned dog washing device can still be found for sale on various online sites and is still being nominated for product and marketing awards.

Yekutiel Sherman also knows all too well what it's like to become a victim of China's lightning-speed copycats. After he launched his Kickstarter campaign (but prior to manufacturing his first unit) of the "*Stikbox*," a smartphone case that turns into a selfie stick, a flimsy, knockoff version, was being sold on AliExpress, at half the price. This just goes to show that your brilliant idea – even if it is patented or trademarked – could be on sale through Chinese distributors even before you've gotten your project funded.

In order to avoid the dog-eat-dog world of manufacturing in China, here are a few top takeaways:

TOP TAKEAWAYS

- File your patents, trademarks and copyrighted images (or videos) in the country you intend to manufacture - prior to sending over your prototypes or drawings.

- Investigate factories prior to engaging them.

- Consider assigning the rights to the factory so that they have a vested interest in protecting your invention from in-house factory thieves.

- Monitor your product online on a daily or weekly basis and report infringing directly on those sites.

- Have eyes on the ground - It may be costly (or impractical) to go back and forth to visit your manufacturer. To ensure that your supplier stays on the up and up, hire a local agent who speaks the language and can easily check on your operations on a routine basis.

- Register your trademarks and copy-rights with U.S. Customs and Border

Protection (CBP) and other foreign ports (e.g., General Administration of Customs in China). This program enables IP owners to block importation of infringing goods if you provide enough information as to what to look for (e.g., detailed information identifying specific manufacturers, importers and consignees of the infringing goods).

"Counterfeiters are a bit like fleas, they itch for a bit, bleed you dry, multiply and then jump onto the next host."

9

ALWAYS RESIST BEFORE YOU CEASE AND DESIST

Do not engage an enemy more powerful than you. And if it is unavoidable and you do have to engage, then make sure you engage it on your terms, not on your enemy's terms.
- Sun Tzu

Sometimes you may find yourself on the receiving end of a Cease and Desist letter - whether it be for trademark, copyright, or patent infringement. Receiving a Cease & Desist (C&D) notice can be alarming, particularly if you didn't *intentionally* do anything wrong. First off, when you receive one of these notices, you are not actually being sued. It is simply a warning to stop doing something and lets you know that further penalties could follow if the behavior doesn't stop. C&Ds are sometimes sent to scare you, though in some instances, you may not need to do anything at all.

The following will help you to resolve your anxiety and to better understand what attorneys are looking for when they examine these issues.

STEP 1: What is the infringing content?

STEP 2: Where is it located (website, packaging)?

STEP 3: Do you own it, or is it someone else's (i.e., did you license it from Shutterstock or did a web developer or marketer create it for you)?

STEP 4: Where is it hosted (your server or someone else's)?

If it's on your server and it's not your content, defenses might apply such as the Safe Harbor which is covered under the Digital Millennium Copyright Act.

Understanding intellectual property bullies requires an appreciation of the differences between patent and trademark law. On one hand, patent owners have the right to exclude others using or selling their invention unless the patent owner grants such rights to a third party and receives a type of royalty payment. However, patent owners have no obligation to exercise that right - they can simply sit on their invention and do nothing with it. If a patent is infringed and the inventor does nothing, his rights to keep his patent are not affected. On the other hand, trademark owners must continuously use their trademarks in order to maintain their rights. In fact, during year 6-7 of having a trademark, one must file a statement that shows such trademark is still in use; otherwise, it will be canceled. Moreover, trademark owners have a duty to enforce their marks to avoid what is called "dilution". As a result, they must continually scour the Internet (or retail shelves) to be sure that no one else is using their trademark.

You may recall the catchy jingle from the Band Aid® commercial -- **I am stuck on Band Aid brand 'cause Band Aid's stuck on me**... (fun fact, this jingle was written by Barry

Manilow, formerly of the BeeGees).

One who is unfamiliar with trademark law might wonder why they didn't just sing, "**I am stuck on Band Aids' 'cause Band Aids' stuck on me**..."

You see, *Band Aid* had to establish their product as a brand because people began to refer to all types of bandages as *Band Aid's*. They did this to avoid dilution of their trademark rights. Other brand names like "*Kleenex*" (as in, "Pass me a *Kleenex*" instead of tissue); "Please make a *'Xerox'* of this" (instead of a copy); and "Who doesn't love a *'Jacuzzi'* (hot tub) party!" In addition, let's not forget our favorite plastic toy disk, the *Frisbee*! In all these instances, their great marketing success turned their brand names into generic names (which can't be protected). Therefore, given the trademark owner's duty to police, it is easy to understand why big companies use such aggressive tactics to prevent trademark infringement.

Just so we are all on the same page here, trademark infringement is when someone uses a brand name, logo, or slogan to trade off the goodwill of an established company. The main test is whether there is substantial similarity such that a competitor's mark *causes* confusion in the marketplace. For example, a beverage manufacturer could not adopt the mark *Koka Kola*, because although this mark is spelled differently from the famous *Coca Cola* mark, it is still pronounced the same and therefore could cause confusion amongst buyers. Trademark law would stop a manufacturer from using the name *Koka Kola* because it would appear to be trading off the goodwill of an existing brand name to promote its products.

If you are on the receiving end of a Cease and Desist notice, it can be intimidating and most small businesses will want to back down right away for fear of getting dragged into court - even if the infringement claims are total malarkey! But must you back down? And if you do back down, do you need to do so right away?

Monster Energy company is famous in legal circles as a "trademark bully" for sending threatening letters whenever a trademark is filed that includes the word "Monster" or an image that includes a monster or a claw-type image. They have bullied over 50 small companies in the past few years, the majority of which settled out of court. Whether or not a party has infringed on another's trademark is a question for the courts, although most trademark infringement cases are settled out of court.

I worked with a product developer in the Philippines who received a C&D for trademark infringement from a large U.S. based company. This case stands out in particular because, if this small client was dragged into court for infringing on a well-known brand, they didn't really have the resources to fight …. Needless to say, we had to get creative.

My client (we'll call them "Blow Up Bed" LLC) called us in a panic -- "We are being sued for trademark infringement and we received a 30-day Cease and Desist letter."

Me: *First, let's be clear. You are not being sued. This is only a threat.*

Him: *But I am looking at the court papers, we are being sued.*

Me: *These haven't been filed. They are just threatening to file those papers if you don't agree to their demand — which is simply to stop using the trademark within 30 days.*

Him: *That's not possible! But…they are a multi-million dollar company. They hired a top NY law firm to handle this. They will crush us.*

Me: *They are just trying to intimidate you. No need to*

blow things out of proportion (pun intended) — let's figure out a strategy.

After reviewing the claims, we told our client this "If you want to defend this trademark it will probably cost you upwards of $100,000 in legal fees; if you lose, in addition to these fees, you may have to hand over all your profits and pay the other side's legal fees as well."

Him: *We'll have to think about this. Then he shared with me something else… Our product is being counterfeited by a Chinese manufacturer using our same packaging and trademark and it's being sold at such a low cost that we can't compete. In any event, we were planning to discontinue this product in a year or so, anyhow.*

At this point, legal light bulb went on. Based on what he told me, we surmised the following:

1) Their remaining life cycle of the product is about one year.

2) The counterfeiter in China affects not only our client, but also the guys threatening to sue us.

Armed with this information, a strategy was formulated. We had leverage as a result of this counterfeiter (as it would be in the other side's best interest to allow us to keep the trademark so we would have the ability to enforce our mark and keep out the counterfeits). We suggested to Blow Up Bed that we negotiate for the rights for 1-2 years of continued use and then we'd agree to abandon the trademark. Our client loved this idea.

We responded to their Cease and Desist letter by suggesting a conference call.

The Negotiations Begin...

ROUND 1:

Started out as friendly conversation and quickly became patronizing.

Them: *Have you any experience representing clients in a trademark action of such magnitude?*

Me: *Sorry, what do you mean by "magnitude?"*

Them: *What I mean is that this is a fairly serious matter. A great deal of money could be at stake for your client.*

Me: *Yes, we read your letter, but it is not clear that you have a valid infringement claim.*

Silence.

Them: *We are authorized to release our claims if your client agrees to cease using its trademark — which is deceptively similar to ours. We can draft up the papers by Monday.*

Me: *With all due respect, the United States Patent and Trademark Office approved our marks 2 years ago. We also have valid trademarks in 9 other countries. You've had every opportunity to file an objection to our registrations before they were granted. How many attorneys do you have over there, anyhow? Isn't someone responsible for tracking these things?*

Tones change. Suddenly, we were being taken seriously.

ROUND 2:

Me: *We conferred with our client, and we agreed to abandon the trademark within 2 years of today's date.*

Them: *This is not an acceptable offer! Are you sure you*

have properly advised your client that large damages are at stake here?

Me: *We will have to seek guidance from our client before we can revise our offer. And then, I sprung this on them: You see, we just discovered that the product bearing the trademark name in question is being counterfeited. This is something that affects us all.*

Sidebar note:

We had just received news that our sales were down as a result of the illegal counterfeiter in China. We began talks with Chinese customs to attempt to seize these goods. *See To Catch a Thief: Intellectual Property Rights in Action (BrillsonLAW, Dec. 12, 2012).*

ROUND 3:

Me: *Gentlemen, we'd like to bring to your attention the grave issue we are addressing with respect to the Chinese counterfeiting I advised you of during our last call. These goods bear our trademark – that same trademark you say is substantially similar to yours. Surely, your client is concerned about this as well. They are currently selling to Big Lots throughout the US.*

Them: *Go on.*

Me: *We are in the process of tracking down these counterfeiters and seizing their goods. It is a costly and potentially lengthy process but one that will benefit us mutually. We have been asked to make a large deposit with Customs in Hong Kong in order to seize these goods. We recommend that we split this deposit.*

Them: *We do not have any instructions from our client in this regard.*

Me: *Either way – it could take up to 2 years to stop this*

production completely. I think you can agree that any efforts on our part to curb this activity would be of mutual benefit.

Them: *Possibly so.*

Me: *Ok. It seems we are close to reaching an agreement.*

Them: *Our client will only agree to a 1-year extension.*

Me: : *Gentlemen, I understand what you are authorized to negotiate, but didn't we just agree that going after the counterfeiters in China would be mutually beneficial?*

Them: *In theory, yes.*

Me: *...and that it could take up to two years.*

Them: *I don't see how this is relevant to our trademark infringement claims.*

Me: *Forgive me if I am missing something here? Doesn't my client need to have a valid trademark in order to pursue the counterfeiters?*

Them: *We will need to discuss this with our client.*

Me: *I will be on extended travel starting tomorrow... Gentlemen, while we prefer to stay away from litigation (only the lawyers win here, hey...chuckle... chuckle), we are pretty confident that our trademarks will be upheld. I will await your reply by end of day or our offer is withdrawn.*

Them: *We will get back to you as soon as possible.*

ROUND 4:

Them: *Our client has agreed to allow you to continue to use the trademark for 2 additional years.*

Me: *Great... 2 years from the date of the signed agreement. Thanks, it's been a pleasure.*

Them: *Um...sorry...but...*

Me: *Gentlemen, sorry to cut you off, but I have a call on the other line...would you like to hold?*

Them: *Um...We will draft up the agreement.*

Now, turning to patent infringement threats; they can be a bit more daunting for two reasons - first, it's a lot more expensive to defend a patent infringement lawsuit, as it requires expert testimony and a more sophisticated analysis of the issues than a trademark action. Second, in many cases, the company that is threatening you is what is commonly known as a patent troll. A patent troll is a company whose main business is to acquire patents (sometimes they buy them in bankruptcy, auction or otherwise) and then sue other companies for infringement. While they used to focus on larger companies, with deep pockets, with all the innovation taking place in Silicon Valley and through local entrepreneurs, small companies have become an easy target. Trolls are frequently successful in obtaining large, recurring license fees in exchange for agreeing not to sue. In fact, upwards of 96% of patent infringement lawsuits settle, many without ever going to court. Small companies may perform a cost-benefit analysis and determine it is cheaper to give in to their demands rather than go to court because even if you've done nothing wrong, they are not going to back off.

If you receive a notice from a patent troll, the worst thing you can do is ignore it, because it doesn't cost them much to prepare a boilerplate complaint and file it, and the next thing you know, you are in a patent infringement litigation. There are a number of tactical strategies that a seasoned IP lawyer can advise you to employ, such as seeking to invalidate their patents at the United States Patent and Trademark Office which will stave off any litigation efforts in the process or checking local statutes to see if the Consumer Protection Act in your state has adopted measures to combat "bad faith" patent infringement claims.

TOP TAKEAWAYS

If you are the recipient of a Cease and Desist letter (which is normally the first step in alerting someone that they are potentially infringing on your intellectual property), here's what to do:

Step One – don't panic.

Step Two – hire counsel with experience in intellectual property before doing anything. Simply responding on the company letterhead is not advisable.

Step Three – break apart scenario and understand the big picture (as in the Blow Up Bed example).

Step Four – perform a cost/benefit analysis.

Step Five – formulate a strategy and take control of negotiations.

And remember…the underdog wins by using an entirely different strategy: Identifying and exploiting their stronger opponent's weaknesses rather than going toe to toe with Goliath.

10 STEALING THE SHOW

Protect against the worst eventualities. Make sure you know what they are." - **Sir Richard Branson**

New inventors, many with a shiny new patent in hand, are eager to display their goods at trade shows with the hopes of attracting a large distributor or retail chain to buy their products. Each trade show normally has a section for newbies – such as Eureka Park at the Consumer Electronic Show – making it very appealing for hungry inventors to showcase their goods. These booths are sold for a lower cost than regular booths, so they are very popular amongst start-up companies. But, little does anyone realize that these trade shows are prime ground for large companies or their agents to replicate their ideas. These undercover roaming attendees frequently hide their badges (or oftentimes, wear fake badges) and sniff around for new ideas. They will typically show some interest and then begin asking questions about costs to manufacture, how many units have you sold, etc. These visitors may even be so bold as to ask for product samples. As first-time exhibitors are untrained as to how to identify these thieves, they are simply lambs to the slaughter.

The problem is so bad, toymaker giant, MGA Entertainment (maker of *Bratz* dolls) once accused Mattel (*Barbie* dolls) of sending spies to its booths at trade fairs and became embroiled in a lawsuit that lasted 8 years. While MGA was the ultimate victor, the only damages it ultimately received was millions of dollars to pay its legal fees. After such a long and drawn out battle, it is no wonder that in 2019, Mattel's booth at the International Toy Show in N.Y. was walled off and security was a tight as U.S. border control.

Having a booth at a tradeshow is not always the wisest choice – particularly if your product has not been patented or your branding has not been trademarked or copyrighted. That doesn't mean that you shouldn't attend. If you have a list of target companies who are registered attendees, reach out to them via email, in advance, introduce yourself and include a short product pitch or attach a product sales sheet. Inquire as to their availability to meet during the show. Most serious buyers are not walking around the trade show floor. Instead, they book executive suites and host private meetings, away from the prying eyes of their competitors.

I attended a consumer products trade show a few years back and one of the exhibitor's – a husband and wife team - proudly displayed their secured delivery bag innovation – a duffle-type bag that would attach to the outside of a person's front door. They explained that "when couriers arrive with a package, they drop the item in the bag; this way no one can steal their packages." The product was brilliantly designed with a catchy logo. They further informed me that "we have a patent pending." When I took a look at the bike lock type mechanism they had rigged up to the bag, I told the husband and wife team to pack up and go home. Naturally they were aghast when I told them that while their idea was probably timely and possibly, quite profitable, there was nothing about that product that was patentable. Husband exclaimed, "The patent protects how the lock affixes to the bag." I explained to him that there are many ways to affix a lock to a bag and all anyone needed to do was to employ a different method of affixing the lock to the bag and they could easily knock off their idea. However, because the product was ready to go I suggested they should identify a distributor who represents similar products and get their item to market as quickly as possible. It warmed my heart to see the couple pack up and go home. The Porch Pirate Bag has become a top seller on Amazon and other retail outlets. Needless to say, there are several other products like this on the market but by taking their "ball" and going home, the couple were able to have a fairly good first mover advantage in the secured delivery bag space.

If you feel confident that you are ready to showcase your goods at a tradeshow, here are a few tips for keeping the competition at bay:

- *Copyright images prior to displaying.*

- *Never discuss pricing on the trade show floor.*

- *Perform due diligence on prospects prior to giving them sales sheet information.*

- *Use closed booths "by appointment only" to vet out potential buyers prior to the show.*

- *If someone refuses to show you their badge, call trade show security and alert them to the matter.*

Lastly, when exhibiting at a show, make sure to have someone in your exhibit space *at all times*; especially if you have high value items laying out like computers, phones, iPads, handbags, etc. Make friends with your booth neighbors who can keep an eye on your booth if you must leave the show floor for a bathroom break, etc.

"What a great, innovative and rare idea! I'll make $$$ selling these!"
CLICK! CLICK! Text Message>> I found a winner to copy<<

11

BUT WAIT!
THERE'S MORE!

He shall not be plagued with lawsuits, have his life shortened and made miserable, and his just right in the property of his discovery snatched from him, if I can prevent it. - Samuel Morse

Guest Submission

Josh Malone, Inventor of Bunch O Balloons®.

The problem is that 99% of inventors are so busy working on their research and development and on commercializing their inventions or getting the prototypes ready or a business plan, that they just assume the patent system is going to work to protect their ideas. I had no idea in 2014 when I filed for my patent that there was any controversy and that no one cares if I have a patent. It was shocking! I thought, *Ok, I got a patent, so, now, they're going to pay attention to me.* Little did I know that the attention that I would receive would be in the form of lawsuits against the biggest infringer in the industry: Telebrands.

By way of background, I quit my job in 2006. I had an

idea I just wanted to pursue and I needed time to focus on it and bring it to fruition. So, I told my wife that I had this invention I wanted to pursue and I was thinking about quitting my job and she was supportive. She thought that it's a good idea; though, she was pretty stunned when three days later, I told her that I actually did quit. Now, we were all betting on this new venture, so I would develop a prototype for a product in the craft and hobby industry and got it working. I took it to trade shows and it turned out, that was actually the easy part. Getting a licensing deal was much harder, so I struggled for about 12 months until I was able to sell a few units to pay some bills and then I went on to my next idea (which was a total flop and I lost a lot of money).

At that point, I went back and dug a little deeper into *Bunch O Balloons*. We decided to scrape together funds and do a Kickstarter campaign. The campaign went viral; it was unbelievable. The first day, it was reported in Gizmodo and then BuzzFeed (if I recall correctly). On the second day, the mainstream media was calling -- *Good Morning America* did a story and then *The TODAY Show* flew me out to New York City. I had a water balloon fight with Carson Daly in Times Square! At that point, my world was just rocking and —there were tons of interest from manufacturers and retailers who wanted me to ship them lots of units.

I was looking at my options at that point. Rather than bring the product to market myself, I wanted to focus on what I'm good at and rely on manufacturers and distributors to bring my product to market. I found a partner called *Zuru*, a family-owned company with a very aggressive and ambitious agenda. They had something very unique, which was automation capability. This was a good thing because manufacturing 37 balloons on a stand at that time was very tedious to assemble using manual labor. With that, I entered into an exclusive manufacturing and distribution agreement with *Zuru* and we went to China to get operations up and running. Walmart wanted to buy several million units and we were busy working to do that properly, and with high quality.

Four months later, my wife received a text message to say that they saw my invention on TV. When she told me this, I said, "I don't think so. It couldn't be my invention; it's too new to be on national TV." With that, I looked it up and, sure enough, the ad featured a product that was an exact copy of my invention; selling under the name *Balloon Bonanza*. I started researching the source of this ad and learned that it was Telebrands, owned by AJ Khubani.

A few days later, I was at church and talking to a friend of mine, and I told him that I got knocked off, it's on TV. The first words out of his mouth were, "It's not AJ Khubani, is it?" I was shocked, how did he guess? I mean there are dozens of these companies, right? and he said, "Oh, Josh, you're in trouble; he's very notorious. This guy is infamous for his ruthless business practices, -- they've written books about him."

Sure enough, I read a few articles, including Ronald Grover's *Infomercial King AJ Khubani*, (Inventors Digest, Feb 2010, p. 4) where he dubbed Khubani as the "Knock-Off King" of the television infomercial industry. I found another exposé of Khubani in the book entitled, *This Business has Legs*, by Peter Bieler (Wiley; May 1996), the marketer behind the mega-successful ThighMaster, which sold over six million units in less than 2 years. Bieler refers to Telebrands as a "Legend in his own time, a knock-off artist par excellence."

At this point, I realized I was in trouble! I shared all this information with my contact at *Zuru* and they immediately sent out a cease and desist letter. Needless to say, the letter was ignored. Nonetheless, we soldiered on, took our product to market, and in 2015, we were selling *Bunch O Balloons®* to Target stores while, at the same time, Telebrands was selling *Balloon Bonanza* in Walmart, and they were trying to put us out of business. I wasn't too surprised, now that I understood what this company did with other products, such as the *Pocket Hose* (knock-off of Michael Berardi's, *Xhose*) and *Ped Egg* (knock-off of Grace Manufacturing, Inc. of Arkansas' *Microplane*).

In fact, I recall seeing the *Pocket Hose* on the shelf right next to the *Xhose* for $9.99, a cheap knock-off that is sold for roughly half the price of the *Xhose* and only lasts for about two or three years, but they don't care. Telebrands does a half billion dollars in these hoses while the inventor couldn't afford to enforce his patent rights. After 16 months of battle, they had to settle.

For my part, I thought we could simply sue Telebrands since we have a patent. I knew we'd have to hire lots of lawyers and experts and we even asked for a preliminary injunction (to get them to stop selling while our lawsuit was underway). Several months later, the order came down and, we won. But that didn't stop Telebrands – they went ahead and flooded the market with as many units as they could. At the same time, they put up a defense to say – not that their product was different but rather, that *my patent should never have been issued*. That's right, they hired an MIT Professor and paid him a bunch of money to argue that my patent should never have been issued. The next thing I knew, my patent was being challenged at the Patent Trial & Appeal Board (PTAB). Telebrands brought their MIT expert to the hearings and the PTAB sided with them and basically canceled my patent! So, on one hand, you have the examiners at the USPTO granting patents and, on the other hand, the PTAB saying their examiners made a mistake and you don't get to keep your patent.

I quickly started working on drafting a new patent application. For those of you who don't know – you can have more than one patent if you are claiming different things. A patent is just a different way of describing the invention; it's like looking at something from different angles (i.e., various view of a 3d object from the top and from back, so that's like having three patents).

So, the same routine started again; Telebrands attempted to invalidate new patents. This time, I had to hire an expert witness who cost us $750,000 to prove economic harm, price collusion, and damage to our brand. By this time, I had spent several million dollars to fight these guys. Telebrands' new defense was that my invention was obvious – "It's just balloons and rubber bands and soda straws," according to the MIT professor's testimony.

Now we were like five million dollars into it. I should point out that while a patent is supposed to grant exclusive rights to the patent owner, we haven't had a day of exclusive rights yet. Meanwhile, the PTAB rules in Telebrands favor again and took away 2 more of my patents. It's just a complete circus that someone can take someone's patented idea, rename it, sell in on TV, and flood the market with cheaper, lower quality products. This time, Telebrands rushed the new product to market so fast (which was somewhat redesigned to avoid infringement) that they ended up using a toxic chemical that was banned by the Consumer Product Safety Commission and consequently, so were the new products. So, while that made them scramble, it didn't matter; they sold junk and they didn't care if they infringed on patents because most inventors couldn't afford to pay millions to sue them. Many people asked me why I didn't just license to Telebrands? Well, the

Xhose, Michael Berardi's expandable hose invention is one of the most (if not the most) imitated products in the history of the Direct Response TV industry; he, too got hosed by Telebrands (pun intended). Although he held 4 patents for his invention (and many international patents), that didn't exclude Telebrands from marketing the widely successful "*Pocket Hose*" nor did it stop TriStar Products, Inc. from selling their similarly successful "*Flex-Able Hose*" knockoffs. Seven years later, lawsuits against TeleBrands and Tristar in the U.S. are still pending the New Jersey's district court's decision.

If all these inventors got slammed by Telebrands and other large marketers like Tristar Products, why should I work with such bullies?

All the while these lawsuits were happening, we managed to sell over 100 million dollars in water balloons. The irony is that we took the profits to pay to the lawyers over the last 4 years and although we spent $20M in litigation, (we've been to the Federal Circuit, the Court of Appeals 13 times) and my patents are still in limbo. I don't even think Apple and Samsung went to court that many times; it just goes to show how bad it's gotten. I don't think many inventors could have survived this kind of attack, let alone pay their bills when they just got started. I've learned from my experience that no one respects patents, or inventors, for that matter.

So, if I win my case after ten years, and millions of dollars spent, inventors will feel like they can't win. The infringer gets to keep the bulk of their profits and give the inventor just a portion of that; that's the current law of the land. After the PTAB found my patents invalid, on Friday August 11, 2017, I participated in an inventors' rights protest, organized by U.S. Inventor, and made a big display of burning my patents on the steps of the USPTO. But that doesn't mean I am giving up the fight.

Whether you have millions to defend a lawsuit or whether you simply chuck up the loss of your patent to a bad experience and move on, I think we can all agree that the Patent Office should do a better job protecting inventors and that no one should be allowed to use a patented invention without permission, and that you shouldn't be able to profit from using a patented invention without permission.

Further, the courts should actually prohibit the infringers from using the invention without permission and not wait for the PTAB to rule on whether they should have granted the patent to begin with. To me, it seems very political – if you are Facebook or Google or Telebrands, you win; if you're an independent inventor, you lose. But that doesn't have to be the case if we independent inventors come together and fight this inequity, which is what we did in forming US Inventor.

US Inventor (https://www.usinventor.org) was formerly founded in 2013 by Paul Morinville, after changes in patent law affected investment in his company; he had basically lost his patents as a result of a Supreme Court decision, *Alice v CLS Bank (573 U.S. 208, 134 S. Ct. 2347 (2014)*. There, the Court determined certain claims about a computer-implemented service for facilitating financial transactions were "abstract ideas" and as such, were ineligible for patent protection. As a result of this decision, many software patents for business patents were subject to scrutiny and ultimately, invalidation.

Paul sold a set of his patents to an investor in 2011 (one of which had already become massively infringed) so that they could manage the litigation and he could use the proceeds to build a company based on the rest of his patents. He started working with the Purdue Technology Center. It took over a year to get the first proceeds to pay for things he needed, and by mid-2013, he began staffing up. By June of 2013, unbeknownst to him, the investor was getting worried and started closing down the licensing campaign. In the beginning of October, he said he was done as soon as the first report of the PTAB patent "kill" rate was over 90%. This killed his revenue stream and, in Paul's words, "I did a bouncing face plant financially." With that, he got in his pickup truck and drove to Washington to tell his congressman the problem, educating over 350 offices about the harm that patent reform was causing to companies like his and others.

US Inventor continues to work to end anti-inventor patent reforms and promotes strong patent rights for inventors. The organization has now 15,000 members and is continuously growing. The main goal of US Inventor is to pass legislation that does three main things: (1) Stop taking back patents from inventors, (2) Prohibit the use of a patented invention without permission, and (3) Prevent profiting from using a patented invention without permission.

We are collecting signatures from thousands of inventors; three inventors from each of the 435 congressional districts. Once you sign the resolution, a member of US Inventor will get in touch to set up a meeting to help deliver the resolution to your representative. You can sign the inventor rights resolution by visiting: www.usinventor.org/resolution/ and completing the form online.

>TACTICS, TIPS & MORE >> PAGES 134 - 136
To read the complete text of 'The Inventor Rights Resolution'

Update: On March 27, 2019, a big win came down for Josh Malone, in the case of Tinnus Enterprises, LLC. v. Telebrands Corporation et al., case number 6:16-cv-00033, in the U.S. District Court for the Eastern District of Texas. The federal judge doubled the jury award and ruled that Malone's company, Tinnus, was entitled to $24.5M plus attorney's fees for Telebrands' infringement of its **Bunch O Balloons** product. The judge found that not only was Telebrand's infringement deliberate and willful but that Telebrand's counsel had engaged in litigation tactics meant to drive up costs of litigation and frustrate the court by repeatedly failing to follow orders. The court also held retailers, including: Bed Bath & Beyond, Fry's Electronics, The Kroger Company, Sears Holding Corp. and Walgreen Co., liable to a portion of the damages for violating the injunction to stop selling Telebrand's knock-off water balloon products, **Battle Balloons**. While this is a promising step forward, the question of whether Telebrands will pay up or appeal the decision remains unknown.

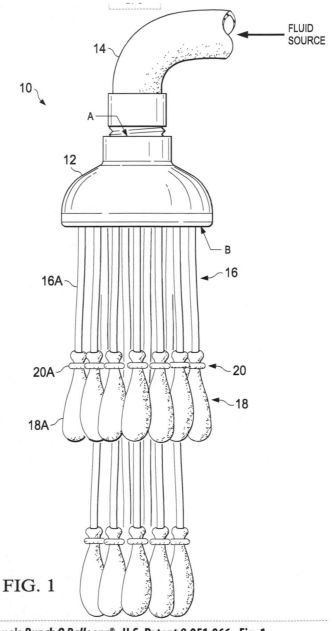

FLUID SOURCE

10

14

A

12

B

16

16A

20A

20

18

18A

FIG. 1

Josh Malone's *Bunch O Balloons®* - U.S. Patent 9,051,066 - Fig. 1

12 | AS STOLEN ON TV

Imitation is the sincerest form of flattery that mediocrity can pay to greatness. - Oscar Wilde

By now, you should have a pretty good picture of the inventing industry as a rough and tumble business and have a better handle on the threats and challenges faced by nearly every inventor. Let's assume for the moment, you *have* done all the right things. You came up with a product that (1) is unique, (2) solves a problem, (3) can be sold at a reasonable price point, (4) has mass market appeal and (5) can be easily demonstrated. Let's also assume that you did not waste thousands of dollars with an invention submission company or an invention school and, instead, smartly invested your capital in intellectual property protection (e.g., patents, trademarks and copyrights), a working prototype, a product mold and that you found a reliable manufacturer. Let's further assume that your product pitch made such a powerful promise that you were able to build a business and begin selling your product or, you were picked up by a reputable distributor who negotiated fair terms (i.e., an advance on royalty, a royalty percentage of at least 3-5%, etc.). By all accounts, you should be well on your path to selling millions of units and achieving the American dream, but...are you?

Guest Submission
Natasha & Fred Ruckel, Inventor's of the Ripple Rug®.

We are a husband and wife team, we live in the Catskills Mountains of NY. One of our businesses is a boutique agency - RuckSackNY – we aim to help to build brands on behalf of small and large companies; from Kickstarter campaigns to Superbowl ads; we've had the opportunity to work on many amazing projects.

Fred had always dreamt of becoming an inventor. Ever since he was young, he'd pull apart gadgets, toys and anything he could get his hands on. He'd then reassemble the item and visualize different applications of dismantled objects; his mind buzzing with ideas of his own.

Fast forward to Valentine's Day 2015. I was composing tunes on the piano while Fred sat listening to me perform and watching our cat Yoda, just six months old, playing with her toys under the wrinkled up drum rug. She poked her paws at her toys in the carpet wrinkles, hooking her play-mice up with her nails, flipping them in the air, then pushing them back under the ripples of the drum rug. As Yoda was fully engrossed in her game of 'cat and mouse,' Fred had a Eureka moment. "We're going to make a *Ripple Rug®.*" The words that sprung from Fred's mouth became the brand name of what would eventually become a number one best-selling cat toy on Amazon.

Filled with hope and excitement, days later, Fred hopped into the car and drove to a home store to purchase different carpet samples and sticky Velcro® strips. He got home, and fabricated a very rough version of the *Ripple Rug*. Fred's first attempt was a disaster; the Velcro didn't stick, the carpet fell apart, the edges frayed, strings were hanging off the edges, carpet fuzzies spread like confetti, the carpet slid across the floor. It wasn't exactly cat safe. Even with those faults, as Yoda expressed an interest in the prototypes, Fred pushed on. After observing Fred struggle with the first mock-ups, I decided to get in on the act; after all, it would be fun to market a cat product, wouldn't it? The next few months, we feverishly sourced alternative materials, conducted construction trials and carpet science research, and even studied cat product behavioral analysis.

As newbie inventors, we were soon overwhelmed, as we discovered the difficulties of sourcing raw materials, safety testing, identifying contract manufacturers, achieving product consistency, and figuring out packaging and shipping costs. We didn't know a lot of people who knew about manufacturing a new product and, as savvy businesspeople, we certainly weren't going to pay thousands of dollars to an "invention consultant." Though, effective, free advice is hard to find, and following a conversation with a family member, it was recommended that Fred should apply for a patent.

Fred looked into the submission and filing of a patent. He learned from Google searches, that creating a 'Provisional Patent' would be a good starting point as it was cheaper to obtain than a full-blown utility or design patent and it would give him time to test product viability and marketability. He felt confident that once he filed for the patent, the "patent pending" notice affixed to each product would be sufficient to deter the bootleggers.

We purchased several (scarily expensive) and rather intimidatingly thick books about writings patents. Learning from the tips included in the patent guides, I went online at google.com/patents and searched for patented cat-products. I read the patents, compared them with suggestions outlined in the books, and attempted to draft a patent for the *Ripple Rug*. Admittedly, I was out of my depth; I had never written anything in such technical 'jargon' before. I chuckled to myself with the number of times the words "embodiments" and "plurality" were used. When it came to writing the 'claims' (arguably, the most important part of the patent application), I realized that a patent attorney would be best suited to draft the non-provisional patent application claims effectively. As it turns out, the claims became pivotal in obtaining a patent.

With the provisional patent in hand, we set up our company, SnugglyCat, Inc. and then created a Kickstarter Campaign to test our idea with a bigger audience. At the same time, Fred submitted an application to appear on *NBC's TODAY's "Next Big Thing,"* an invention competition. Somehow we made the cut and were selected as finalists on the Show. Fred and I were overjoyed to be selected to appear on *NBC*; we knew our idea had the potential to propel the *Ripple Rug* to the masses, A link to *The TODAY Show*, featuring their product pitch, can be found here:

www.youtube.com/watch?v=IpYzPb0S0yI.

Unbeknownst to Fred and myself, our appearance on *NBC* (which was run in conjunction with a QVC cross promotion), let the cat out of the bag! We didn't think for a moment that these airings were being seen by unscrupulous actors. We soon learned that an employee of 'Rutledge & Bapst,' a Connecticut based marketing company, decided to pinch the idea and create a national TV campaign, with the aim of creating a *Ripple Rug* knock-off.

Nonetheless, we continued to push the sales of the *Ripple Rug*. It soon become a number one best seller on Amazon, as well as a most wished for product. The sales were growing significantly, and Christmas 2016 was on track to be a best seller with record sales.

However, coming up to Black Friday, sales suddenly diminished and, it wasn't until I looked at our *Ripple Rug* Amazon listing that I noticed all but one of the photographs had been removed. The accompanying text and most of our bullets had also been removed. I initially thought Fred had removed all this information, as no one else had access to our Amazon account. Of course, Fred hadn't removed anything, but that certainly wouldn't explain why sales had diminished. As it turned out, another 'seller' took control of our listing and removed all the pictures, graphics and all descriptive bullets and information; essentially sabotaging our campaign. Although we sent a subpoena to Amazon (requesting the identity of the vendor that took control of our listing), the results were of no use. The seller was a fake business listing with an incorrect business address and the bank information was seemingly a pre-paid anonymous credit card. Whoever was sabotaging our listing had covered their tracks and had a reason for doing so.

Around February 2017, a friend of ours, Dan Shultes, came to visit Fred for his birthday and told him that someone mentioned to him that they saw our television commercial, however, it was called something else. Fred was puzzled, *"TV commercial? We didn't have a budget for TV*!!" Turns out, the product being sold on TV featured our identical product, though, it was sold under the name 'Purr N Play.' We were in shock and disbelief; not only were the counterfeiters trying to sell a knock-off, but they also had the audacity to use the actual *Ripple Rug* in the *Purr N Play* (knock-off) commercial.

Fred decided to analyze the video of the *Purr N Play* in closer detail, frame by frame. After hours of scrutiny, this tedious exercise paid off. Fred came across several frames, in which a cute black kitten (playing and having a jolly good time), rolled the top carpet away and, to his surprise, the *Ripple Rug* woven label was revealed. Not only were the counterfeiters trying to sell a knock-off, but they also had the audacity to use the actual *Ripple Rug* in the *Purr N Play* commercial.

We quickly embarked on a several-month long investigation. After locating the *Purr N Play* website, we jotted down the name of the company that built the website – Digital Target Marketing. As it turns out, Digital Target Marketing are experts at creating websites for Direct Response advertising and, are used by many 'As Seen On TV' organizations. There's a good chance that if a product has been launched - the folks at Digital Target Marketing may have been paid by third-party parasites to create a website, to test market the cheapo twenty-buck version of your beloved product. As a third party vendor, Digital Target Marketing has no liability for the provision of their services so then, who was responsible?

We continued to analyze the *Purr N Play* video. We were looking for other clues that would help us identify the studio or the middle-aged women who provided testimonials in the *Purr N Play* TV Commercial. I recall how disappointed I was that two seemingly cat-loving women would lie, claiming that "their cats loved the *Purr N Play*." It made my blood boil; I wished that, if I could ever meet those women in person, I'd share with them how upsetting, unfair and dishonest their actions were.

Driven by our disgust of the bad players, we started searching for "shopping channel" type studios. The *Purr N Play* commercial was clearly shot in a studio-shopping-style set-up. We decided to focus their efforts on finding that particular set. Fred finally stumbled upon an email from a company called,

"*The Bargain Show.*" *The Bargain Show* solicits inventors in order to offer their services. Fred managed to track *The Bargain Show* back to a company in Springfield, Missouri named Opfer Communications. On visiting the Opfer Communications website and Facebook pages our suspicions were confirmed, several other product commercials had all been shot in the same studio set as the *Purr N Play* commercial.

As you can imagine, Fred repeatedly contacted Scott Opfer (the owner and Founder of Opfer Communications) but got no response – just crickets (or, as Fred says, "*just cowards*").

Meanwhile, we continued our investigations and searched for casting calls for both middle-aged women and cats. While going through the Facebook feed of Opfer Communications and posts by their employees, I came across a post requesting '*a litter of kittens who would like to be stars in front of camera.*' My investigations uncovered not only the actual kittens featured in the *Purr N Play* commercial, but also the two women who delivered the testimonials. One of the testimonials was provided by Opfer's own producer, Krissi Bernhardi. Yes - an actual employee of Opfer Communication provided a testimonial. It makes you wonder how many of these testimonials are real these days? "*What type of unethical production company uses their own employees as 'genuine' spokespersons for knock-off products?*" asks Fred.

I was also curious to discover if the other products featured on *The Bargain Show* website were also knock-offs. Having conducted significant searches using Google and, in particular, Amazon, I was able to identify similar products to those featured on *The Bargain Show*. These products had different names and were seemingly created by American 'mom and pop' inventors.

I found what I believed to be the original inventors'

websites and gave the information to Fred so that he could-follow up and contact those people directly.

Fred continued to reach out to other inventors whose products had been copied and then featured on *The Bargain Show*. Some inventors weren't even aware that *The Bargain Show* was selling knock-offs of their product. One of the knock-offs featured on *The Bargain Show* website was the *Spyder Sprinkler*, a knock-off of the **Noodlehead Sprinkler**. However, when Fred reached out to speak to Randy Cooper (through the contact information provided on the Noodlehead website), Fred was saddened to learn that Randy had passed away a few years prior.

After performing a great deal of research about inventors' rights and possible causes of action to file a lawsuit against the infringers, and, after sending a strongly worded Cease & Desist notice, in March 2017, SnugglyCat Inc. (our company), filed a lawsuit against Rutledge & Bapst. As is the case, with a large percentage of unscrupulous individuals, they'll deny everything, delay decisions, avoid answering queries, and flat out lie while dragging the proceedings on with the goal of bleeding inventor's resources. A lawsuit is costly, both emotionally and financially while consuming all your time.

We learned, during part of the 'discovery' phase of our lawsuit, that just one month of launching our product on *The TODAY Show* (September 2015), one of Rutledge & Bapst's employees, Laurie Bieber, purchased a *Ripple Rug* from QVC, as in her words, "*It's more anonymous that way.*" (Note: QVC was NBC's partner for the "*TODAY's Next Big Thing*" competition). It turns out, Laurie Bieber purchased subsequent *Ripple Rug*s from QVC, which were later sent to a Chinese manufacturer to make knock-offs, and they used the actual *Ripple Rug* product and pictures in their knock-off commercial. In the course of our research, we found out that several other products were being exploited in much the same way including: *Mighty Shower* (a knock-off of the original **Thunderhead**) and *Draft Defender* (a knock-off of the original **Evelots Magnetic Clip On Door Draft Stopper**). It became clear that companies, such as Rutledge & Bapst were mere "*feeders*." They sourced other people's products, test marketed them and, if they tested well, they would 'license' the knock-off products to larger marketers who then go on to sell the product on Amazon, in catalogs (on and offline), and in the "As Seen On TV' section in big box stores.

What we surmised was that once a potential "hot" product is advertised, Rutledge & Bapst then checks to see if there is a patent. If the patent hasn't been issued yet, they proceed to work with companies, such as Digital Target Marketing, to create a test website that uses images from the original products but changes the brand name (to avoid trademark infringement). In our case, they stole images from the *Ripple Rug* website as well as our QVC product listing. This test website was found by accident, as it was hidden from Internet bots (i.e., to avoid being catalogued in a Google search). The purpose of these test sites is to blast marketing emails to a targeted list with the goal of getting consumers to place an order for the products. The *Purr N Play* email blast was sent to a targeted audience of **over 960,000** people.

The recipients who visited the site saw pictures of our cat, Yoda, loving her *Ripple Rug* and all the marketing language presented was lifted directly from our *Ripple Rug* website. If that was not offensive enough, the *Purr N Play* was being advertised at 75% below the *Ripple Rug's* advertised price. Clearly, anyone who compared the two products side by side would think it was the exact same product and, with one being 75%

less than the other, it's not difficult to predict which product would sell the most rugs. It's hard to quantify the impact this would have had on *Ripple Rug* sales, because as a new company, there was no sales history to cross-reference, only continued growth, until this caper took place (this proved to be the biggest obstacle in proving damages in a lawsuit that later ensued).

We later discovered that Ron Steblea, President of Rutledge & Bapst, approached Scott Opfer, President of Missouri based Opfer Communications, to enter into a partnership for marketing the fake product called the *Purr N Play;* sharing equally in all profits. Scott Opfer signed on as a full partner and committed to producing and shooting a commercial for the *Purr N Play* in return for his 33 1/3 percent of sales.

Fast forward two years later, we successfully settled a lawsuit against Rutledge & Bapst and then filed suit against Scott Opfer, Opfer Communications and their employees – a lawsuit which we pursued until our funds were depleted via 'motion practices' employed by Opfer Communications and it's legal counsel.

Any start-up company, going up against a larger company, backed by their insurance company and a highly aggressive lawyer (think, Atilla the Hun) who ratchets up the billable hours, takes a fair amount of capital. We intend to resume our efforts once we rebuild our business and replenish our resources. Fred says, *"I will never be done going after the bad guys of this industry. I want them put out of business, jailed or both."*

The bad guys have deep pockets. They use funding from the profits of selling knock-offs, or they buy hefty insurance policies to cover 'wrongful acts' that unbelievably agree to fund the defense of their unlawful activities. As a small business, the toll you pay can be prohibitive. It may even seem to many that the justice system defends 'he who has the biggest purse strings.' Where is the justice for the newbie inventor whose ideas and consequently, sales, have been stolen by thieves hiding in plain sight under the anonymity of the Internet and "fake" Amazon sellers?

Having fought the battle against knock-offs, unscrupulous infringers, spineless arbitragers, slap-dash manufacturers, fake-reviewers, phony bloggers, unlawful marketers, etc., we decided to take this knowledge and form the Randy Cooper Foundation (RCF). Thus, a non-profit organization to support home-grown inventors was born. The foundation was named after Randy Cooper, the inventor of the *Noodlehead Sprinkler*, in honor of his spirit of innovation.

Founded in 2018 by Natasha, Fred and myself, RCF aims to provide an ethical, low-cost alternative to invention submission companies or inventing schools. The Foundation's goal is to uphold Randy's honesty and integrity by protecting, educating and empowering inventors. Visit AsStolenonTV.com website (randycooper-foundation.org) to learn more about how RCF supports innovation.

ASIDE NOTE FROM PAULA: What the Ruckels encountered is certainly not a stand-alone situation and not unlike many others, they did not have the resources to defend their intellectual property rights and their products are simply 'STOLEN ON TV'.

"Just because you caught me red-handed with my paw in the cookie-jar doesn't mean I did anything wrong. I didn't get to eat a single crumb!"

TACTICS, TIPS & MORE: IMPROVE YOUR RESULTS

Guest Submission

3 KEYS TO INVENTING SUCCESSFUL NEW PRODUCTS™
Authored by Eric P. Rose, NPDP, MBA

I have been tinkering, inventing, engineering, and launching new products since 1980 and teaching this subject in Southern California universities since 2009. I have worked with individual inventors like Michael Boehm, the inventor of the George Foreman grill (no, it wasn't George who invented it). I have also worked with the world's largest toymaker, Mattel. I have seen a number of people create their own invention process to try and make sense out of what is often a crazy sequence of fits and starts and oftentimes failures. I argue that it doesn't have to be quite so crazy.

Although most inventors start by focusing on the product's design, it's actually better to work on your invention after you know what the problems are with existing products. Many inventors prefer to skip this market research step because they are "sure" they know what the market needs. I've had some inventors tell me that their mother loved their invention!

I've developed a simple 3-step program I call, "**3**

Keys to Inventing Successful New Products™." I created this process in 2012 after seeing so many inventors, entrepreneurs, and startups struggle to understand the basics of the invention process. My approach simplifies the process down into the following 3 "Keys" written in the order they should be done. They are:

1.) Marketability

2.) Technical Feasibility

3.) Protectability

Marketability is the first and most important key in my invention process, (even if your mother says she already loves your idea). About 70% of my clients haven't done enough market research to justify spending money on the product development and patent protection work they have already done or are about to do. Market research involves a number of steps, but most importantly, it should start with interviewing the "stakeholders." Stakeholders are the end users, distributors, retailers, and opinion leaders who would have contact (or otherwise license or use) with your new product. These interviews are best done face to face (not just via email or online surveys). Interviews are also best done using an interview guide; a list of objective questions about what type of problems the stakeholders have seen or experienced using similar products that are already being sold. Once these interviews are completed, the results are studied to figure out if there is a clear, overwhelming, and most importantly a consistent message of what the stakeholders want the new product to do; in other words, marketability. These results are what you'll use for the next stage -- your product development work -- which I call, "Technical Feasibility."

**Technical Feasibility** is where the inventor determines whether the product can be designed, engineered, and manufactured at a cost low enough so that everyone in the distribution channel can make a profit. This technical work is done using the results from the first key, marketability. But, beware! Inventors love to invent (I know because I spent the first half of my career as an inventor/engineer), but the end game here is not beautiful engineering, it is creating something of value to the customers who will buy or perhaps license your new product. You can use a rule of thumb here to figure out the maximum amount the invention should cost to produce. This will get you to a "Target Manufacturing Cost."

That rule of thumb would look like:

**Retail product sell price: $20**

**Manufacturer's selling price to retailer: $10**

**Target Manufacturer's Cost**
**(parts, labor, outbound shipping if prepaid): $5**

**Protectability** is the final "Key" after you've concluded that there is a market for your new product, and you have figured out that it's technically feasible, then you will want to protect your new product with a "blanket of intellectual property" and other methods. This would include design and utility patents, trademarks, and copyrights. While many inventors try to file their own patents, I do not recommend this.

I suggest that inventors write a detailed "invention disclosure" for their patent attorney. This would include information on what products are already out in the market that compete with yours and why exactly, in detail, yours is better. This Invention Disclosure should also include a description of how the product would actually be made. This would include both written descriptions and drawings of your product in enough detail so the patent attorney will understand your thinking about how the product could be made.

CONCLUSION

I know your invention is your "baby." However, the most important aspect of inventing is delivering value to those who will buy or license your product. So, if you follow my 3 Keys to Inventing Successful Products™, the odds of you being successful is significantly increased. Remember to focus your initial efforts on the market research, actually interviewing stakeholders face to face. After interviewing 30 or more stakeholders, you will learn so much about what is valued in the market and how your invention needs to be designed. Once that's complete, you can move on to the fun part of designing and prototyping your invention (Technical Feasibility), and lastly, once the prior two Keys are completed, reach out to a patent attorney to guide you through protecting your invention.

MARKETING RESEARCH & COMPETITOR ANALYSIS

You can't do market research/competitive analysis too early; here is some insight into a typical investigation process:

1) Name and Email Address Searches: Use popular search engines to research individuals/company names and email addresses (best if you have both their business and personal email addresses). If the company has a list of partners or shareholders, search their names and emails too.

2) Reverse Look Up Phone Numbers: Use www.whitepages.com or fonefinder.net and see if the registered name appears. Then enter the phone numbers, e.g., "111-555-1212". Running this search gives you a good idea if the phone number has been used anywhere online.

Sidebar Note:
Sometimes you find a different name other than what they provided as the registered user, or you may find a website where the phone number or email was used as a contact number. From there, you may even find a personal ad placed where the subject was offering employment or seeking investment. You can also find out which forums the subject hangs out at and read their comments.

3) Patent/Trademark Searches: Go to the USPTO.GOV website and see if the person is associated with any trademark or patent filings. In one case, we learned that an individual making detailed inquiries into a company was in fact representing a competitor and was posing as a potential customer, trying to find out confidential information from my client.

4) Domain Name Searches: *Go to www.betterwhois.com and see if this person/company owns any by searching the "whois" directory to see if credentials check out. If a website is soliciting inventions, but the "whois" data is private (that is, you don't know the owner of the website), for all you know, you could be sending your ideas to a counterfeiter in China!*

5) Business Registration Searches: *Go to the Secretary of State's website in the company's place of incorporation. Do a business entity search and see whether the company is in good standing (e.g., is the company paid up on taxes and registration fees?) and who the shareholders are, if listed.*

7) Civil/Criminal Records Search: *Go to the website of the county/state to search online for civil and criminal records on the subject. You can find out which county to search based on the subject's phone number or zip code revealed in the previously mentioned searches.*

8) Keyword Searches: *Prior to signing any agreements with a third party, Google their name along with keywords such as "scam," "complaint," or even "invention scams."*

There is always the case that your research turns up nothing at all! Then what? My advice is to ask for recommendations or referrals; ideally from someone you or someone you trust have done business with. Failing that, walk into any big box store (e.g., Walmart, Target, Walgreens) and go to the section that carries your category of goods. For example, if you invented a cooking product, go to the cookware section and select a product. Take out your phone and take a photo of the UPC code. You can then find out the source of the product. Visit their website - do they represent a wide range of products in your category? If you think they may be a good fit - reach out to the other inventors they represent (e.g. via LinkedIn or email) and check whether they have lawsuits filed against them? Do they have a history of settling cases for infringement? You owe it to yourself to be as careful as possible in selecting your business partners, as it may make the difference as to whether you will ever see a dime of your royalties.

*Consumer Complaint Websites - Go to sites such as:

http://www.complaintsboard.com

http://www.complaints.com

INVENTOR RIGHTS RESOLUTION*

*(*As referenced by Josh Malone in Chapter 11)*

Our patent system is in crisis. Recent changes to patent laws and Supreme Court decisions have adversely affected inventors such that the requirement in Article I, Section 8 of the Constitution of "securing for limited times to inventors the exclusive right to their discoveries" is no longer achieved. It is nearly impossible to stop an infringer from using an invention without permission, or to make them to pay for the damage caused when they do. The undersigned inventors call on Congress to pass legislation to address these critical issues.

PTAB – The USPTO Must Stop Taking Back Patents From Inventors

Patents that are infringed are often contested in the Patent Trial and Appeal Board (PTAB), which is an administrative tribunal within the USPTO, purported to be an alternative to traditional federal courts, and created by the 2011 America Invents Act. To defend a patent costs the inventor several hundred thousand dollars, and usually cannot persuade the PTAB to uphold the patent. Even if the inventor prevails in the first challenge, others are allowed to challenge the same patent over and over again. This has been devastating to inventors and small businesses that rely on patents to protect investments and build businesses. Participation in PTAB reviews should be voluntary at least while the patent is held by the original inventor. If PTAB reviews become a fair alternative to validity challenges in a traditional federal court, then inventors will participate voluntarily. Otherwise, patents that are believed to be invalid can be contested in a traditional federal court, as has always been the case.

INJUNCTIONS – Courts must prohibit use of a patented invention without permission

In the 2006 eBay decision, the Supreme Court held that in most circumstances a patent cannot prevent an infringer from using the invention. For instance when a large corporation can produce the invention faster, cheaper, or in greater quantities, they are allowed to keep selling in perpetual violation of the patent. Thus the inventor has no say in who gets to use the invention and what they do with it. The inventor cannot determine the price, the quality, the brand, the features, the materials, the factory location, the working conditions, environmental sustainability, or any other concern. Indeed, the inventor is compelled to grant the infringer a license for a royalty amount determined by the court. The eBay decision should be overturned, and the court should issue an injunction ordering the infringer to stop using the invention until they have obtained a license negotiated in good faith with the inventor.

PROFITS – Infringers must not profit by using an invention without permission

Current law limits most inventors who win in court to only a "reasonable royalty", which in many cases does not cover legal fees and is too little to serve as a deterrent against large corporations with deep pockets. Large corporations simply ignore patents, knowing that few inventors can afford the millions of dollars and many years required to enforce their patents in court. In the rare case that an inventor survives the legal gauntlet, the infringer usually is ordered to share only a small percentage of their profits with the inventor while keeping the rest for themselves. Without penalties infringing is much more profitable as a business strategy than inventing. To restore fairness and respect for patents, infringers should not be allowed to keep their profits made from someone else's invention.

For the full resolution with signatures, please visit:
www.randycooperfoundation.org/resolution

PRIOR ART: ARE YOU YOUR OWN WORST ENEMY?[1]

When you consider whether or not you have an idea worthy of patent, you're likely to think about what others have done -- has another person come up with the same idea already? Am I just re-inventing the wheel? What is seldom considered is whether or not our own actions jeopardize our right to obtain a patent.

In daily practice, your own actions may be more damaging to your ability to obtain a patent than anything else. For instance, a perfectly novel, patentable idea (an invention) that is disclosed to the public prematurely, may prevent an owner from patenting and protecting that invention from infringement years later. It seems strange (and a bit unfair) that your own actions to promote your invention could jeopardize your ability to protect it, but it is true.

An idea can be patented only if it is new, non-obvious and useful. Public use and disclosure, printed publications, sales or offers for sale, or any act that makes an idea "otherwise available to the public" is called prior art. Prior art can take many forms, and anyone can create prior art, even an inventor.

Various forms of advertising and public use such as can constitute prior art, including:

~ YouTube Videos ~ Promotional Materials ~
Trade Show Demonstrations ~ Blog Posts ~ Crowdsourcing Sites ~

Additionally, if you are manufacturing a product, contracting with a foreign manufacturer to make your product is considered a sale. Once a sale has been made, or even the offer to make the sale occurs, you need to take actions to protect your invention.

---

1   *Reprinted with permission; Digital Law Group blog (2014) (co-authors Paula Brillson Phillips & Jessica Sutherland).

ABOUT THE AUTHOR

Paula Brillson Phillips has built her career advising start-up companies and mentoring hundreds of individual inventors worldwide to navigate the complex process of getting a business or product off the ground. She also works directly with executives to help them make effective decisions to protect their intellectual property, meet their business goals, and leverage the value of what they have already created. Paula also acts as a Mentor to young entrepreneurs through Peter Thiel's 20 Under 20 Foundation.

Paula is the Managing Partner of Digital Law Group, LLP. She received her J.D. from Rutgers Law School in 1993.

For more than 20 years, she has successfully navigated hundreds of small businesses through the legal hurdles they face in starting and running their businesses. She represents clients in investigative and enforcement proceedings brought by the Federal Trade Commission, state attorneys general, district attorneys, and other federal and state agencies with jurisdiction over advertising and marketing practices. Paula also manages outside counsel in complex litigation cases against infringers.

GLOSSARY

- A -

Advertising Cost of Sales (ACoS): A metric used to measure the performance of an *Amazon Sponsored Products* campaign. ACoS indicates the ratio of ad spend to targeted sales and is calculated by this formula: Ad spend ÷ sales = ACoS.

Adjusted Gross Revenue: Total revenue derived from the sale of goods or services less allowable deductions and/or set offs.

Allowable Deductions: Includes business and/or operating expenses that may be deducted prior to calculating a royalty percentage owed to a licensor.

America Invents Act (AIA): Also known as Leahy–Smith America Invents Act. Passed in 2011, the Act, among other things, switched the U.S. rights to a patent from the previous "first to invent" system to "first to file" system for patent applications.

American Inventors Protection Act of 1999: Passed in 1999 to protect inventor rights by establishing a cause of action for inventors injured by materially false or fraudulent statements or representations, or any omission of material fact, by an invention promoter, or by the promoter's failure to make the required written disclosures as set forth more fully in the statute.

Allegation of use (AOU): This applies to trademarks filed on the basis of a 1(b) *Intent to Use*. The applicant must submit a specimen showing use of the mark for each class of goods/services included in the application. If the specimen is filed after the mark is approved, the AOU is also called a Statement of Use.

Application (patent): An application for patent filed naming the inventor and must contain: a specification, claim(s), drawings (when required) and an oath or declaration stating that the applicant is the actual inventor; along with the required filing fees.

Application filing date (trademark): The date the USPTO receives a fully completed application along with the required filing fees.

Application number (patent): The unique number assigned to a patent application when it is filed. The application number includes a two digit series code and a six digit serial number.

Arbitration: An alternative method of resolving disputes through various tribunals (e.g., American Arbitration Association or JAMS) including mediation and arbitration.

Assignee: The entity that is the recipient of a transfer of a patent application, patent, trademark application or trademark registration from its owner of record (assignor).

Assignment (agreements): A clause included in an agreement which states whether either party to the agreement may assign its rights to a third party and whether the other party must consent prior to any such transfer of rights.

Assignment: A transfer of ownership by the "assignor" of a patent application or patent or a trademark application or a trademark from one entity (or person) to another "assignee". Assignments are with the USPTO Assignment Services Division to become a matter of public record to establish the Assignee as the owner.

Assignment (agreements): The transferring of rights (such as website operations or Amazon store) for the duration of licensing or distribution agreement to a third party to enable them to perform their duties under the agreement.

Assignor: The owner of a patent application, patent, trademark application or trademark registration or domain name who is transferring (assigning) ownership to another (assignee).

- B -

Boilerplate: A legal slang for provisions in a contract that are standard or routine.

Bait and Switch: Advertising tactic that lures buyers in with a compelling offer and then then tries to sell them a substitute item by telling them the original offer is no longer available.

- C -

Call to Action (CTA): The portion of a DRTV commercial asking the viewer to place an order. Often used term is 'Call Now' or 'Act Now' in order to take advantage of the advertised offer.

© **Copyright Registration Symbol**: The symbol used in copyright notices for works other than sound recordings.

Cancelled: A trademark registration that is inactive due to failure to respond to an office action or to pay maintenance fees.

Cancellation proceeding: A proceeding before the TTAB where the plaintiff attempts to cancel a mark's registration on the basis that the registration will harm or damage the goodwill of the plaintiff.

Certificate of registration: Official document bearing the USPTO seal evidencing that a mark is registered at the USPTO.

Certification mark: A mark filed by members of a union or organization that is used to show origin of goods, material, , quality, or other characteristics of the goods or services.

Claims: Specification of the invention.

Classification of goods and services: An international system used to classify the category of goods or services that will be sold under a particular trademark.

Clearance search: A search of names that is performed prior to filing a trademark application to ensure that the chosen mark is available for use and registration.

Click-through rate (CTR): The ratio of users who click on specific links to the number of total users who view a webpage, blog, email, or advertisement as compared to those who receive the link but do not click through.

Coinventor: Where more than one inventor contributes to the creation of an invention (i.e., develops one or more claims) that is included in a patent application.

Collective mark: A mark that is used by members on an association.

Confidentiality Agreement (Non-Disclosure Agreement): Protect information shared with an employee, client, vendor or other party.

Continuation: A second application for the same invention that is filed before the first application is granted or abandoned which includes additional claims.

Conversion Rate: The percentage of leads (i.e., visitors to a website or viewers of an infomercial) that turn into sales.

Copyright Office: A division of the Library of Congress that maintains records of copyright registrations filed within the United States.

Country of origin (trademark): The country where a trademark applicant resides or is incorporated.

Cost of Goods: The direct costs associated with manufacturing and packaging of a product (i.e., including raw materials, freight or shipping charges).

Cost per order: Also referred to as CPO ratio refers to how much media you are spending to generate a single order. For example, if you spend $100,000 in Media and generate 5000 orders, the CPO is calculated as $100,000/5000 orders, which equals $20.00. *See also* MER.

Current filing basis: The designation of a trademark as not yet in use but intended to use (§1(b) filing) or is already in use in commerce (§1(a) filing).

- D -

Descriptive mark: A mark that only describes the products or services such as its ingredients, qualities, features, purpose or characteristics will be refused registration on the basis that it lacks distinction (e.g., Big Book or Hot 'n Spicy Chicken).

Design around: *See* Work Around.

Design Patent: Intellectual property protection granted for a novel and unique ornamental design (e.g., a shape of a bottle or eyeglass design) which is granted for a period of 14 years.

Design patent application: An application for a patent

to protect against the unauthorized use of new, original, and ornamental designs for articles of manufacture.

Digital Millennium Copyright Act: Defines legal duties with which Internet Service Providers (ISPs) must comply in order to limit their legal liabilities in the event a user of their service violates copyright laws (including providing the identity of the infringer in response to a subpoena).

Disclosure: In return for a patent, the application fully describes the invention they seek to protect.

Distributor: A company or agent that undertakes to supply goods to stores and other businesses that sells to end-users on another's behalf.

Distribution Channel: Refers to the means of offering a product for sale be it retail, wholesale or direct to consumer via various means such as internet or TV advertising.

Domestic Representative: Refers to a person residing within the United States who represents an applicant who lives or resides outside the country.

Drawing (patent): Schematic of each feature of the invention that is specified in the claims.

Drawing (trademark): An application must include either standard characters (words) or a drawing of applied-for the mark (logos, and/or colors (if claimed as a feature of the mark)).

DR Media Agency: A company which buys infomercial or short form media on behalf of a client and provides reports on profitability of Long Form or Short Form commercial airings for a customary fee of 15% of the billings.

DRTV – Direct Response Television: Any television (or digital) advertising that asks consumers to either visit a website or call an 800 number to make a purchase.

- E -

EFS-Web: Electronic Filing System - web-based filing system to upload applications and other data to the USPTO website.

Efficient Infringement: Deliberate infringement of a patented or trademarked product where a cost-benefit analysis deems it cheaper to infringe (and possibly pay damages) than to obtain a valid licensing agreement.

Enforceability of patent: The ability of a patent owner to bring an infringement action against someone who, without permission, makes, uses or sells a patented invention during the life of the patent plus six years.

Examiner's amendment: An amendment made to a trademark application by the examining attorney following consultation with the applicant.

Examining attorney: A USPTO attorney assigned to review trademark applications.

Expired: Trademark registration is no longer active due to a failure to renew the mark at the end of registration period.

Express abandonment: A written declaration submitted to the USPTO that the trademark will no longer be used.

Extension Request: A sworn statement signed by the applicant stating applicant has a good faith intention to use the mark in commerce, and needs additional time to show proof that the mark is in use accompanied by the required fees.

- F -

False advertising: False or misleading statements about a product or service's source, benefits or origin. To bring a claim for False Advertising (Section 43(a) of the Lanham Act), requires that a plaintiff show (1) defendant made false or misleading statements as to his own products (or another's); (2) actual deception; (3) deception influenced purchasing decisions; (4) the advertised goods are transported in interstate commerce; and (5) a likelihood of injury to plaintiff. *See also* Bait and Switch.

Feeder: A person or company which seeks out products for marketability and feeds them to a marker in a process known as *Flipping*. (*See* Flipping).

File Wrapper: A complete record of proceedings in the USPTO from the filing of the initial patent application to the issued patent.

Filing basis: The legal basis for filing an application for registration of a mark which mainly fall into 3 categories including: (1) use in commerce under (§1(a) filing); (2) intention to use a mark in commerce under (§1(b) filing); (3) based on an previously-filed foreign application.

Filing date: The date the USPTO receives a completed an application along with the required filing fees.

First Sale Doctrine: When a copyright owner has sold a lawfully made copy of his or her work, the purchaser is permitted to transfer, distribute or lend that copy to another person without violating copyright or trademark laws.

Flipping: The act of gathering all testing data (target market, price points, etc) to demonstrate product appeal in order 'Flip' product to someone else (normally in exchange for a fee).

Freight on Board (FOB): A shipping term used to describe the time when the supplier or seller is no longer responsible for the shipped goods and when the buyer is responsible for paying the transport costs (e.g. FOB China port or China factory).

- G -

GDRP (The General Data Protection Regulation): European Union law passed in May 2018 that sets forth policies regarding data collection and privacy to safeguard personal information on the internet.

Gross Revenue: Total revenue derived from the sale of goods or services.

- I -

IC: International Class: Refers to the classification of goods and service that are assigned to a trademark.

Identification of goods and/or services: A written statement of the goods or services included in an application. Every application must include an identification of goods and/or services.

Incontestability: Under Section 15 of the Trademark Act, a trademark may be declared incontestable after five years of continuous means which means that it can never be cancelled through Trademark Trial and Appeal Board proceedings.

Indemnification: An agreement to receive compensation for loss incurred as a result of a specific incident. An example is where an inventor indemnifies a licensee in the event the invention is found to infringe on another patent and the infringer is ordered to pay damages.

Infringement (patent): To make, use, sell or offer to sell, any patented invention without the permission of the patent owner or licensee.

Infringement (trademark): To use a trademark on or in connection with goods or services in a manner that is likely to cause confusion, deception, or mistake about the source of the goods or services.

Intellectual property: Refers broadly to patents, trademarks, copyrights or trade secrets.

Intent to use: Refers to a trademark application filed Section 1 (b) of the Trademark Act where the mark applied for is not yet in use with regard to the sale of any goods or services. Once the trademark is actually in use, the applicant must file a Statement of Use in order to obtain registration of the mark.

Invalidation: An action to oppose an application for a trademark (after registration) before the Trademark Trial and Appeal Board (TTAB).

Invention: Any art or process *(way of doing or making things)*, machine, manufacture, design, or composition of matter, or any new and useful improvement thereof, or any variety of plant, which is or may be patentable under the patent laws of the United States.

Inventor: One who contributes to the conception of an invention. The patent law of the United States of America requires that the applicant in a patent application must be the inventor.

IP: Intellectual property

Issue date: The date that a patent application becomes a US patent. The USPTO issues patents on Tuesdays.

- J -

Joint application (joint inventors): An application in which the invention is presented as that of two or more persons have contributed to the invention set forth in at least one claim in a patent application.

Jurisdiction: Refers to the court or tribunal that has the authority to interpret and apply the law with respect to a particular legal or administrative matter.

- L -

Licensee: The entity that has contracted to license the rights to sell a product to wholesalers, retailers and/or consumers.

Licensor: The entity owning the rights to the product that contracts to license its rights to a third party.

Likelihood of confusion: A basis for rejecting a trademark application when an applied-for mark is similar to another mark so much so that it may cause confusion as to the source of the goods or services.

Liquidated Damages: Refers to damages that would be paid to an injured party in the event a contract is breached.

Long Form: Refers to an infomercial that is either 30 or 60 minutes in length.

- M -

Madrid Protocol: An international treaty that allows trademark owners to register in other countries that are members of the treaty by filing a single application, called an "international application."

Maintenance fees (renewal fees): Refers to the fees that are paid to the USPTO or other foreign patent office for maintaining patent rights. Maintenance fees are due at the fourth, eighth and 12th-year anniversary from the time the patent is granted.

Mark: *See* trademark.

Media Buy: Purchasing advertising from a media company (i.e., TV station, newspaper, magazine, blog or website) to convey a marketing message to a target audience.

MER (Marketing Expense Ratio or Media Efficiency Ratio): Refers to how much revenue a campaign is generating against a particular media spend. For example, if you spend $100,000 in media and generate 5000 orders, the MER is calculated $200,000/$100,000, which equals a 2.00 MER.

Market Research: A method used to research a market to determine the demand for a product conducted using various means such as direct response advertising, local sales channels, in-person interviewing, direct sales results and feedback from potential buyers.

Mechanical Drawing: Illustrations that are submitted as part of a patent filing that depicts the functionality of the invention.

Mere descriptiveness: *See* Descriptive mark.

- N -

Net Media Billings: Shall mean all media costs charged by any broadcast or cable entity to advertisers for commercial airings (including the media agency fees).

Net Revenue: Gross (total) revenue, less costs and expenses.

Non-Compete Agreement: In contracts, a non-compete clause prevents a party from enter into a similar business or selling a competing product for a specified term.

Non-Disclosure Agreement (NDA): *See* Confidentiality Agreement.

Non-final office action: Refers to an Office action letter that raises issues that may prevent a trademark from being registered unless the applicant responds within 6 months from the date of issuance otherwise, the application will be considered abandoned.

Nonprovisional patent application: An application that the specifications along with claims or drawings; an oath or declaration; and the required filing fee.

Notice of abandonment: A written notification from the USPTO that an application has been deemed abandoned as a result of failure to respond to an office action or to pay fees. The applicant has 2 months from the issue date to revive the application or request a reinstatement of the application.

Notice of allowance (NOA): A written notification from the USPTO (following publication in the Official Gazette) that a mark that was applied for under Section 1(b) "intent to use" has survived the opposition period and will be allowed registration. After receiving a NOA, the applicant must file a statement of use (or a request for an extension of time to file) within 6 months from the date of the notice.

Notice of publication: A written statement from the USPTO notifying an applicant that its mark will be published in the Official Gazette and if no objections are filed within 30 days from the date of publication, the examining attorney will approve the mark for publication.

- O -

Office action: A letter from the examining attorney assigned to a trademark application which normally requires a response from the applicant in order for the trademark application to continue to process.

Office of origin (trademark): The government trademark office in a country that is a member of the Madrid Protocol.

Opposition proceeding: An action to oppose an application for a trademark (prior to registration) before the Trademark Trial and Appeal Board (TTAB).

- P -

PAIR (Patent Application Information Retrieval): Electronic means to patent application status online.

Passing off: Falsely representing another's product as one's own (e.g., selling another's product under a different name) or using copyrighted images of another to promote one's own product.

Patent pending: A phrase that often appears on manufactured items. It means that someone has applied for a patent on an invention that is contained in the manufactured item. It serves as a warning that a patent may issue that would cover the item and that copiers should be careful because they might infringe if the patent issues. Once the patent issues, the patent owner will stop using the phrase "patent pending" and start using a phrase such as "covered by U.S. Patent Number 0000000." Applying the patent pending phrase to an item when no patent application has been filed can result in a fine.

Patentable: An idea that is novel, useful, and nonobvious is suitable to be patented.

PCT (Patent Cooperation Treaty): Is an international patent law treaty that enables an applicant to file a single application to seek patent protection in various countries that are members of the PCT.

PCT Regulations: Provide rules concerning matters expressly refers to in the Patent Cooperation Treaty, any administrative requirements, matters, or procedures, and concerning any details useful in the implementation of the provisions of the Patent Cooperation Treaty. The rules must be adopted by the Assembly of WIPO.

Petition to revive an application (trademark matters):

a formal request for the USPTO to return an abandoned application to active status.

Principal Register: Primary trademark register of the USPTO. When a mark has been registered on the Principal Register, the mark is entitled to all the rights provided by the Trademark Act.

Priority claim (patent): A claim an applicant makes under 35 U.S.C. §119(a)-(e) and 35 U.S.C. §120 to receive the benefit of the filing date of an earlier-filed application(s).

Provisional patent application: Refers to a type of patent application that is submitted without formal patent claim(s) or any information disclosures (prior art) which is effective for a period of 1 year. It allows the term "Patent Pending" to be applied to a product.

Product Category: Defines a product based on use and market. For example, games fall into the toy category, cleaning supplies are under household goods, supplements and beauty creams fall under health and beauty, etc.

PTAB: The Patent Trial and Appeal Board. Conducts trials, including inter partes, post-grant, and covered business method patent reviews and derivation proceedings, hears appeals from adverse examiner decisions in patent applications and reexamination proceedings, and renders decisions in interferences.

PTO: Patent and Trademark Office, former designation for USPTO.

Publication for opposition: A trademark is published in the Official Gazette once the examining attorney has approved the mark for registration. Any party who wishes to oppose the mark has 30 days from the publication date to file either an opposition (or request an extension of time to oppose).

Publication number: A number assigned to the patent applications filed on or after November 29, 2000.

- R -

Recordation form cover sheet: Form used to transfer (assign) ownership of registered trademarks and trademark applications.

Reexamination proceeding: During the enforceability of a patent, any person may file a request for the USPTO to conduct a second examination of any claim of the patent on the basis of prior art patents or printed publications. In order for the request for reexamination to be granted, a new question of patentability must be raised with regard to at least one patent claim.

Refusal: A USPTO Office action which states the final determination of a trademark application.

Registration: Federal registration of trademarks evidencing registrant's claim of ownership of a Trademark.

Registration number: Refers to a number assigned by a registered patent attorney/agent that must be included on all correspondence to the USPTO.

Renewal Fees: *See* Maintenance Fees.

Reverse Engineering: Taking apart a specific product to figure the process used to manufacture or develop it.

Rough cut: A first stage version of an edited commercial or infomercial.

Rollout: Refers to a product release that is introduced to the general public via TV, social media ads or print ad campaigns.

Royalty: A payment made by a licensee to the licensor for selling a product; usually pursuant to terms of a pre-negotiated agreement.

- S -

Section 1(a) applications: If you file a trademark application with this basis, you must actually be (a) using the mark you want to register with the goods and/or services in an application, (b) this use must be in commerce, and (b) prior to or at the time of filing an application. You will need to submit proof of how you actually use the mark.

Section 1(b) applications (intent-to-use basis/ITU): Refers to a trademark application that the applicant intends to use.

Section 15 Declaration of Incontestability: *See*

Incontestability.

Section 8 Declaration of Continued Use: A sworn statement, filed by the owner of a registration that the mark is in use in commerce which must be filed at the end of the 6th year after the date of registration and at the end of each 10-year period after the date of registration.

Serial number: A number assigned by the USPTO to an application at the time of filing.

Sell Off Period: Period provided for at the end of a license or distribution agreement during which the licensee can sell existing inventory and stock, or fulfil existing orders. Also known as a run-off period.

Short Form: Refers to a video or infomercial that is 30 seconds to 1 minute in length.

Service mark: A word, name, symbol or device that is to indicate the source of the services and to distinguish them from the services of others. A service mark is the same as a trademark except that it identifies and distinguishes the source of a service rather than a product. The terms "trademark" and "mark" are often used to refer to both trademarks and service marks.

Set Off: Refers to an amount that may be deducted from royalties owed (e.g., advance payment on royalties, chargebacks, product recalls or product returns).

Small (or Micro) entity: Means an independent inventor, a small business concern, or a nonprofit organization eligible for reduced patent fees.

SOU: (Statement of Use): *See* Notice of Allowance.

Special form drawing: *See* Stylized Mark.

Specification: A written description of the invention and the manner and process of making and using the same.

Specimen (trademark): An image submitted as part of a trademark application that shows the applicant's mark in use in connection with the goods or services. For a trademark, acceptable specimens include: labels, tags, packaging, or containers for goods or webpages. For a service mark, acceptable specimens include: advertising and marketing materials such as webpage advertisements or direct mail or email advertising.

Standard character drawing: Refers to a type of trademark that includes words only – without any reference to a particular font style, size, or color or design

State trademark registration: Protects your trademark in the state where you register it. Generally used for products or services that are sold within the state only or products that are legalized in particular state(s) but not on a federal level (e.g., cannabis products).

Statement of use (SOU): *See* Notice of Allowance.

Stylized mark: Refers to a trademark application that contains stylized lettering, a design or logo, and/or color. An applicant must submit a specimen of the exact applied-for mark along with a description of the mark.

Supplemental register: Refers to registration of marks that do not meet all the requirements for registration on the Principal Register but are still capable of distinguishing an applicant's goods or services. Marks registered on the Supplemental Register do not qualify for incontestability.

Suspension letter: An application may be suspended for a variety of reasons until a particular issue is resolved.

- T -

TARR: Stands for Trademark Application and Registration Retrieval system operated by the United States Patent and Trademark Office (uspto.gov).

Trademark Application: A filing to request a federal trademark registration. An application must include (1) the applicant's name, (2 address for correspondence, (3) a clear drawing of the mark sought to be registered, (4) a list of the goods or services, and (5) the application filing fee and (6) a specimen (if the mark is already in use).

Trademark Document Retrieval (TDR) system: Free online retrieval of documents and files on the USPTO website for trademark applications and registrations.

Trademark Electronic Application System (TEAS): USPTO's electronic filing system. It may be used to file a patent or trademark application, change address or contact information, record assignment documents and respond to Office Actions, just to name a few.

Term of art: An expression or phrase that has a defined meaning when used in a particular context.

TESS (Trademark Electronic Search System): USPTO's free online database for searching registered and applied for trademarks.

Trade dress: A product's design, product packaging, color, or other distinguishing nonfunctional element of appearance.

Trade secret(s): Information that companies keep secret to give them an advantage over their competitors.

Trademark: Protect words, names, symbols, sounds, or colors that distinguish goods and services from those manufactured or sold by others and to indicate the source of the goods. Trademarks, unlike patents, can be renewed for as long as they are being used in commerce.

Trademark Symbols: The use of the symbol ™ after the mark itself means the trademark is unregistered ; use of the symbol ® means that the mark has been registered with the USPTO or foreign trademark office.

Trademark Manual of Examining Procedure (TMEP): Contains information about the trademark examination process, and outlines the procedures which examining attorneys are required or authorized to follow in the examination of trademark applications.

Trademark Status and Document Retrieval (TSDR) System: An online system that will retrieve documents from the USPTO's electronic case file for any federal trademark or service mark applications and/or registrations that you own.

TTAB (Trademark Trial & Appeal Board): an

administrative tribunal that has jurisdiction over trademark appeals, opposition and cancellation proceedings.

TV Test: Producing an infomercial and airing on television to gauge product demand. A TV test is performed after a successful web test and upon a successful TV test a product goes into to 'Rollout' stage.

- U -

Upsell: Any product or service offered for sale as an add-on or upgrade which is generally advertised as free (other than the cost of the shipping and handling).

Use in commerce: For the purpose of obtaining federal trademark registration, the mark must be used in the ordinary course of business. For goods, the mark must appear on the goods and/or packaging of the goods which are sold or transported. For services, the mark must be used or displayed in connection with the sale or advertising of the services.

USPTO: United States Patent and Trademark Office.

Utility patent: Intellectual property protection granted for the functionality aspects of a product, process, machine, manufacture, or composition of matter, or any new and useful improvements to an existing invention which is granted up to a period of 20 years.

- V -

VeRO: The Verified Rights Owner (VeRO) program allows owners of intellectual property (IP) rights and their authorized representatives to report eBay listings that may infringe on those rights.

- W -

Web Test: An online marketing campaign that is performed for the purpose of testing market demand, determining buyer demographics or the effectiveness of marketing campaign.

WIPO (World Intellectual Property Organization): An intergovernmental organization of the United Nations. WIPO is responsible for protecting intellectual property and administrating various multilateral treaties as it relates to the legal and administrative aspects of intellectual property.

Work-Around: To create or "to design around" a patented invention that does not infringe on the original patent.

Word mark: A type of trademark comprised of text only.

INVENTOR ORGANIZATIONS

The following inventor groups and organizations may be useful for new inventors connect with experienced inventors during the initial stages of inventing. The author is neither endorsing nor recommending any of the organizations listed below.*

STATE ORGANIZATIONS (Arranged in Alphabetical Order by State)

Alaska Inventors & Entrepreneurs
Pam Middaugh
P.O. Box 241801
Anchorage, AK 99524-1801
Tel: (907) 563-4337
E-mail: inventor@arctic.net

Invent Alabama
Bruce Koppenhoefer
137 Mission Circle
Montevallo, AL 35115
Tel: (205) 663-9982

Inventors Association of Arizona
Lisa Lloyd
P.O. Box 12217
Tucson, AZ 85732-2217
Tel: (520) 751-9966
Toll Free: (888) 299-6787
Tel (Phoenix Office - Linda Schuerman):
(800) 299-6787
E-mail: Arizona-Legal@Juno.com

Inventors Alliance
Andrew Krauss
P.O. Box 390219
Mountain View, CA 94039-390219
Tel: (650) 964-1576
E-mail: president@inventorsalliance.org

Contra Costa Inventors Club
Sherm Fishman
295 Stevenson Drive
Pleasant Hill, CA 94523-4149
Tel: (510) 934-1331

Bruce Sawyer Center
Charles Robbins
520 Mendocino Avenue, Suite 210
Santa Rosa, CA 95401
Tel: (707) 524-1773

Inventors Institute of Alaska
Al Jorgensen
P.O. Box 876154
Wasilla, AK 99687
Tel: (907) 376-5114

Inventors Congress Inc.
Garland Bull
Route 2 Box 1630
Dandanell, AR 72834
Tel: (501) 229-4515

Inventors Forum
Scott Gilzean - President
P.O. Box 8008
80 Huntington Street, #9
Huntington Beach, CA 92615
Tel: (714) 253-0952
E-mail: info@inventorsforum.org

Central Valley Inventor's Assn.
John Christensen
P.O. Box 1551
Manteca, CA 95336
Tel: (209) 239-5414
E-mail: cdesigns@softcom.net

San Diego Inventors Group
Greg Lauren
11190 Poblado Road
San Diego, CA 92127
Tel: (858) 673-4733

American Inventor Network
Jeff McGrew
1320 High School Road
Sebastopol, CA 95472
Tel: (707) 823-3865

Idea to Market Network
Sidnee Cox
P.O. Box 12248
Santa Rosa, CA 95406
Tel: (707) 838-6967
Toll-Free: (800) 486-3210
E-mail: info@ideatomarket.org or
sidnee@ap.net

**Rocky Mountain Inventors
Association**
Roger Jackson, Esquire
209 Kalamath Street, Unit 9
Denver, CO 80223
Tel: (303) 271-9468
E-mail: info@RMinventor.org

Innovators Guild
Hal Meyer or Robin Faulkner
52 Bank Street, Suite A
New Milford, CT 06776-2706
Tel: (860) 350-2709
E-mail: pro@thehooktek.com or
RFaulkner@snet.net

Inventors Society of South Florida
Robert L. Levy, President
P.O. Box 244306
Boynton Beach, FL 33424-4306
E-mail: boblevy@bellsouth.net
Tel: (305) 205-2884 or (305) 893-5989

Tampa Bay Inventors Council
David Kiewit
5901 Third Street South
Saint Petersburg, FL 33705-5305
Tel: (813) 866-0669
E-mail: webmaster@patent-faq.com

Space Coast Inventors Guild
Angel L. Pacheco, Sr.
1221 Pine Tree Drive
Indian Harbour Beach, FL 32937
Tel: (407) 773-4031

Inventors Forum Chapter in Whittier
Anthony Harris
14034 Oval Drive
Whittier, CA 90605
Tel: (562) 464-0069
E-mail: info@inventorsforum.org or
anthonyh@inventorsforum.org

Inventors Association of Connecticut
Pal Asija
7 Woonsocket Avenue
Shelton, CT 06484
Tel: (203) 924-9538
E-mail: iact@inventus.org or pasija@
cs.com

Delaware Entrepreneurs Forum
Colleen Wolf
P.O. Box 278
Yorklyn, DE 19736
Tel: (302) 234-4440

Edison Inventors Association, Inc.
Gary Nelson
P.O. Box 07398
Fort Myers, FL 33919
Tel: (941) 275-4332
E-mail: drghn@aol.com

Inventors Council of Central Florida
David Flinchbaugh
4855 Big Oaks Lane
Orlando, FL 32806-7826

Inventor Associates of Georgia, Inc.
Ron Reardon
3356 Station Court
Lawrenceville, GA 30044-5674
E-mail: rreardon@bellsouth.net

Drake University Inventure Program
Ben Swartz
SBDC-Drake University
2507 University Avenue
Des Moines, IA 50311
Tel: (515) 271-2655

Inventors' Council
Don Moyer
431 South Dearborne, #705
Chicago, IL 60605
Tel: (312) 939-3329
E-mail: patent@donmoyer.com

Inventor's Council of Cincinnati
Andrea Brady, President
121 Bradford Drive
Milford, OH 45150
Tel: (513) 831-0664
E-mail: InventorsCouncil@fuse.net

Inventors Council--Wabash
2783 East Old 24
Wabash, IN 46992
Tel: (219) 782-2511

Mid-America Inventors Association
David Herron
P.O. Box 2778
Kansas City, KS 66110
Tel: (913) 371-7011
Email: midamerica-inventors@kc.rr.com
www.midamerica-inventors.com

East Idaho Inventors Forum
John Wordin
P.O. Box 452
Shelly, ID 83274
Tel: (208) 346-6763
E-mail: wordinjj@ida.net

Illinois Innovators & Inventor's Club
Phil Curry
P.O. Box 623
Edwardsville, IL 62025
Tel: (618) 656-7445
E-mail: invent@charter-il.com

Indiana Inventors Association
Robert Humbert
5514 South Adams
Marion, IN 46953
Tel: (765) 674-2845
E-mail: arhumbert@busprod.com

Inventors Association of South-Central Kansas
Richard Friedenberger
2302 North Amarado Street
Wichita KS, 67205 -1526
Tel: (316) 721-1866
E-mail: richardf@inventkansas.com

Central Kentucky Inventors& Entrepreneurs
Mohamed H. Nasser
117 Carolyn Drive
Nicholasville, KY 40356
Tel: (606) 885-9593
E-mail: nashky@ibm.net

Cape Cod Inventors Association
Ernest Bauer
Briar Main -- P.O. Box 143
Wellfleet, MA 02667
Tel: (508) 349-1629

Worcester Area Inventors
Barbara Wyatt
132 Sterling Street
West Boylston, MA 01583
Tel: (508) 835-6435
E-mail: barbara@nedcorp.com

Inventors Clubs of America
Carl Preston
524 Curtis Road
East Lansing, MI 48823
Tel: (517) 332-3561

Inventors Council of Mid-Michigan
Bob Ross
519 South Saginaw, Suite 200
Flint, MI 48502
Tel: (810) 232-7909
E-mail: lcmm@bigfoot.com or
LFORD22649@aol.com

Minnesota Inventors Congress
Deb Hess, Executive Director
235 South Mill Street
P.O. Box 71
Redwood Falls, MN 56283
Tel: (507) 627-2344
E-mail: mic@inventhelper.org

**Greater Boston Inventors Association
(Inventors Association of New
England)**
Robert Hausslein
20 Slocum Road
Lexington, MA 02173
Tel: (978) 533-2397
E-mail: crholt@aol.com or starco@juno.
com

Innovators' Resource Network
Dave Cormier and Karyl Lynch
Pelham West Associates
P.O. Box 137
Shutesbury, MA 01072-0137
Email: info@IRNetwork.org
Website: www.IRNetwork.org

Portland Inventors Forum
Jake Ward
Dept Industrial Co-op
University of Maine
5717 Corbett Hall
Orono, ME 04469-5717
Tel: (207) 581-1488
E-mail: jsward@maine.maine.edu

Inventors Club of Michigan
Tom Milgie
24685 Ravine Circle, Apartment 203
Farmington Hills, MI 48335
Tel: (810) 870-9139

Society of Minnesota Inventors
Paul Paris
P.O. Box 252
St. Francis, MN 55070
Tel: (763) 753-2766
E-mail: paulparis@uswest.net

Inventors' Network
Bill Baker
23 Empire Drive, Suite 105
St. Paul, MN 55103
Tel: (612) 602-3175

Mid-America Inventors Association
Carl Minzes
8911 East 29th Street
Kansas City, MO 64129-1502
Tel: (816) 254-9542

Society of Mississippi Inventors
Dr. William Blair
3825 Ridgewood Road
Jackson, MS 39211
Tel: (662) 915-5001
E-mail: blantrip@olemiss.edu or blair@
IHL.state.MS.US

Montana Inventors Association
Casey Emerson
5350 Love Lane
Bozeman, MT 59178
Tel: (406) 586-1541

Lincoln Inventors Association
Roger Reyda
92 Ideal Way
Brainard, NE 68626
Tel: (402) 545-2179

Inventors Society of Southern Nevada
Penny J. Ballou
Las Vegas, NV
Tel: (702) 435-7741
E-Mail: inventssn@aol.com

Women's Inventor Project
Betty Rozier
7400 Foxmount
Hazlewood, MO 63042

Inventors Association of St. Louis
Robert Scheinkman
P.O. Box 410111
St. Louis, MO 63141
Tel: (314) 432-1291

Yellowstone Inventors
Warren George
3 Carrie Lynn
Billings, MT 59102
Tel: (406) 259-9110

Northern Plains Inventors Congress
Contact: Michael S. Neustel (Neustel Law Offices, LTD.)
2534 South University Drive, Suite 4
Fargo, ND 58103
Tel: (701) 281-8822

Nevada Inventors Association
Tony Patti
P.O. Box 11008
Reno, NV 89510-1008
Tel: (775) 677-4824
E-mail: rvrdl@aol.com or costar@ibm.
net

New Hampshire Inventors Association
John Rocheleau
P.O. Box 2772
Concord, NH 03302-2772
Tel: (603) 228-3854
E-mail: john@nhinventor.com

Jersey Shore Inventors Club
Ed McClain
416 Park Place Avenue
Bradley Beach NJ 07720
Tel: (732) 776-8467
E-mail: emcclain@injersey.com

New Jersey Entrepreneurs Forum
Jeff Millinetti
P.O. Box 313
Westfield, NJ 07090
Tel: (908) 789-3424

Inv. Alliance of America-Buffalo Chapter
Mark Ellwood
300 Pearl Street
Olympic Towers, Suite 200
Buffalo, NY 14202
Tel: (716) 842-4561
Email: ellwood@netcom.ca

Inventors Alliance of America -
Rochester Chapter
Jim Chiello
97 Pinebrook Drive
Rochester, NY 14616
Tel: (716) 225-3750
E-mail: InventNY@aol.com

Inventors Council of Cincinnati
TJ Tully
3178 Victoria Avenue
Cincinnati, OH 45208
Tel: (513) 321-7280 or (513) 772-9333

National Society of Inventors
Shelia Kalisher
94 North Rockledge Drive
Livingston, NJ 07039-1121
Tel: (973) 994-9282

New Mexico Inventors Club
Albert Goodman
P.O. Box 30062
Albuquerque, NM 87190
Tel: (505) 266-3541

NY Society of Professional Inventors
Daniel Weiss
P.O. Box 216
Farmingdale, NY 11735-9996
Tel: (516) 798-1490

Inventors Network of Greater Akron
John Sovis
1741 Stone Creek Lane
Twinsburg, OH 44087
Tel: (330) 425-1749

Inventors Connection Greater Cleveland
David Hitchcock
P.O. Box 360804
Cleveland, OH 44136
Tel: (216) 226-9681
E-mail: icgc@usa.com

Innovation Alliance
Nicola Harmon
2000 Henderson Road, #140
Columbus, OH 43220
Tel: (614) 326-3822

Inventors Council of Canton
Frank Fleischer
303 55th Street Northwest
North Canton, OH 44720
(330) 499-1262
E-mail: president@inventorscouncilof
canton.org

Inventors Council of Greater Lorain
Henry Ferguson
1101 Park Avenue
Elyria, OH 44035
Tel: (216) 322-1540

Oklahoma Inventors Congress
P.O. Box 0204
Edmund, OK 73083-0204

American Society of Inventors
Jay Cohen
P.O. Box 58426
Philadelphia, PA 19102-5426
Tel: (215) 546-6601
E-mail: hskillman@ddhs.com

Northwest Inventors Council
Robert Jordon
Gannon University
Erie, PA 16541
Tel: (814) 871-7619

Inventors Network, Inc.
Bob Stonecypher
1275 Kinnear Road
Columbus, OH 43212
(614) 470-0144
E-mail: 13832667@msn.com

Inventors Council of Dayton
George Pierce
P.O. Box 611
Dayton, OH 45409-0611
Tel: (937) 293-2770
E-mail: geopierce@earthlink.net

Youngstown-Warren Inventors Association
Bob Herberger
500 City Center One
P.O. Box 507
Youngstown, OH 44501-0507
Tel: (330) 744-4481
e-mail: mm@cisnet.com

South Oregon Inventors Council
Nancy Hudson
SBDC@ South Oregon State
332 West 6th Street
Medford, OR 97501
Tel: (541)772-3478

Pennsylvania Inventors Association
Jerry T. Gorniak
2317 East 43rd Street
Erie, PA 16510
Tel: (814) 825-5820
E-mail: jgorniak@pa-invent.org

Inventors Council - Pittsburgh
David S. Gilbert, Jr.
110 Rock Run Road
Elizabeth, PA 15037
Tel: (412) 751-6545

Carolina Inventors Council
Johnny Sheppard
2960 Dacusville Highway
Easley, SC 29640
Tel: (864) 859-0066
E-mail: john17@home.com

**Inventors' Association of Middle
Tennessee
and South Kentucky**
Marshal Frazer
3908 Trimble Road
Nashville, TN 37215
Tel: (615) 269-4346

Houston Inventors Association
Chuck Mullen
2916 West T.C. Jester Boulevard, Suite 105
Houston, TX 77018
Tel: (713) 686-7676
E-mail: kenroddy@nol.net

**Network of American Inventors
& Entrepreneurs**
Alison McCaleb
P.O. Box 667113
Houston, TX 77006
Tel: (713) 523-3923
E-mail: info@naie.org

**Inventors Network of the Capital
Area**
Bill Kuntz
P.O. Box 15150
Arlington, VA 22202
Tel: (703) 971-9216
E-mail: info@inca.hispeed.com

Tennessee Inventors Assn.
Dewey Feezell
P.O. Box 11225
Knoxville, TN 37939-1225
Tel: (865) 539-4466
E-mail: bealaj@aol.com

Amarillo Inventors Association
Paul Kiefer
7000 West 45th
Amarillo, TX 79105
Tel: (806) 352-6085

Laredo Inventors Association
Jorge Guerra
210 Palm Circle
Laredo, TX 78041
Tel: (956) 725-5863

Texas Inventors Association
Marry Russell Sarao
2912 Trophy Drive
Plano, TX 75025
Tel: (972) 312-0090

**Association for Science, Technology &
Innovation**
Robert Adams
P.O. Box 1242
Arlington, VA 22210
Tel: (703) 241-2850

Blue Ridge Inventor's Club
Richard Britton or Mac Woodward
P.O. Box 7451
Charlottesville, VA 22906-7451
Tel (Richard): (804) 973-0276
Tel (Mac): (804) 973-3708
E-mail: hetex@juno.com

Inventors Network of Vermont
Dave Dionne
4 Park Street
Springfield, VT 05156
Tel: (802) 885-8178 or (802) 885-5100
E-mail: comtu@turbont.net

Northwest Inventors Guild
Stan E. Delo
P.O. Box 226
Port Hadlock, WA 98339
Tel: (360) 821-5919 or (360) 385-6863
E-mail: aero1@waypt.com

Whidbey Island Inventor Network
Matthew Swett or Sarah Birger
P.O. Box 1026
Langley, WA 98260
Tel: (360) 321-4447
E-mail: wiin@whidbey.com

Inventors Network
Rick Aydelott
P.O. Box 5575
Vancouver, WA 98668
Tel: (503) 239-8299

Tri-Cities Enterprise Assn.
2000 Logston Boulevard
Richland, WA 99352
Tel: (509) 375-3268

CANADA

**Inventors Alliance of Canada/America
- Toronto & Buffalo, NY Chapters**
Mark Ellwood
47 Kenneth Avenue
Toronto, ON M6P 1J1, Canada
Tel: (416) 410-7792
E-mail: ellwood@netcom.ca

Inter Atlantic Inventors Club
Tomas Romero
28021 Tacoma PO
Dartmouth, NS Canada B2W 6E2
Tel: (902) 435-5218

Saskatchewan Research Council
Marie Savostianik
15 Innovation Boulevard
Saskatoon, SK Canada S7N 2X8
Tel: (306) 933-5400

UNITED STATES

United Inventors Association (UIA)
1025 Connecticut Ave, Ste 1000
Washington DC 20036
Email: admin@uiausa.org

Other Countries: See International Federation of Inventors' Associations
Website: ifia.com

Reprinted with permission from National Inventor Fraud Center, Inc. (inventorfraud.com)

"I didn't steal the idea - *honest gov* - I came up with it all by myself.
I didn't troll early morning TV and see any inventors present products!"

BIBLIOGRAPHY

"Joy Mangano." Wikipedia. April 25, 2019. Accessed May 04, 2018. https://en.wikipedia.org/wiki/Joy_Mangano.

"Minority Student Program." Rutgers Law. January 09, 2019. Accessed May 04, 2019. https://law.rutgers.edu/minority-student-program.

Harris, Graham. "How To Make Your Idea The One-In-5,000 That Actually Makes Money." Minutehack. May 14, 2018. Accessed May 30, 2018. https://minutehack.com/guides/how-to-make-your-idea-the-1-in-5000-that-actually-makes-money.

Rose, Eric P. "3 Keys to Successful New Products." Lecture, Protecting Your Invention - Panel Event, Sherman Oaks Galleria, Sherman Oaks, March 3, 2019.

Yapp, Roderic. "George Foreman Become World Champion at 44." Leadership Forces. February 13, 2017. Accessed May 04, 2018. https://www.leadershipforces.com/george-foreman-became-world-champion-44/.

Sundt, Hal. "A Tale of Two Grill Masters." *Inventors Digest,* Vol. 31, No. 5 (May 2015): 18-24.

American Inventors Protection Act of 1999, Pub. L. No. 106-113, 113 Stat. 1501 (First Inventors Defense Act codified at 35 U.S.C. § 273(b)(1) (2000)): 15-17.

"InventHelp Disclosure Process." Inventhelp. May 23, 2017. Accessed May 04, 2019. https://inventhelp.com/leadPages/ uploads/PDF/InventHelp_Affirmative_Disclosure_05232017- 8e33-867b-e017-3856fd58ee94.pdf.

"Submit Your Idea." Davison. Accessed May 04, 2019. https:// idea.davison.com/index.php.

"World Patent Marketing." Enforcement; Cases and Proceedings. May 30, 2018. Accessed May 04, 2018. https:// www.ftc.gov/enforcement/cases-proceedings/172-3010/ world-patent-marketing.

Brown, MacKenzie. "Invention Marketing Companies: Don't Get Scammed." Cad Crowd. Accessed May 04, 2018. https://www. cadcrowd.com/blog/invention-marketing-companies-dont- get-scammed/.

"Invention Promoter and Promotion Firm Complaints." Invention Promoter and Promotion Firm Complaints. Accessed May 2019. https://www.uspto.gov/patents-getting-started/ using-legal-services/scam-prevention/published-complaints/ published: 26, 91-92

"HOME." The Randy Cooper Foundation. Accessed May 04, 2019. http://randycooperfoundation.org/.

"Making Money From Your Patent." Eligibility. January 15, 2019. Accessed May 04, 2019. https://eligibility.com/patents/making-money-from-your-patent.

"Why Corporate Advocacy." RipOffReport. May 4, 2019. Accessed May 4, 2019. https://www.ripoffreport.com/corporate-advocacy: 91-92.
"Ripoff Report." Wikipedia. September 20, 2018. Accessed May 04, 2019. https://en.wikipedia.org/wiki/Ripoff_Report.

Press Release, The White House Office of the Press Sec'y, President Obama To Sign Jumpstart Our Business Startups (JOBS) Act (Apr. 5, 2012) *available* at http://www.whitehouse.gov/the-press-office/2012/04/05/president-obama-sign-jumpstart-our-business-startups-jobs-act.

"Crowdfunding Industry Statistics 2015 2016." CrowdExpert.com. January 12, 2016. Accessed May 01, 2018. http://crowdexpert.com/crowdfunding-industry-statistics/.

"Pluck N' File - More than a Tweezer (Suspended)." Kickstarter. December 5, 2014. Accessed May 01, 2018. https://www.kickstarter.com/dmca/pluck-n-file-more-than-a-tweezer-suspended-submitted-by-assoulin.

"Vince Offer." Wikipedia. April 30, 2019. Accessed May 01, 2018. https://en.wikipedia.org/wiki/Vince_Offer.

TheSlapChop. "Slap Chop." YouTube. July 18, 2009. Accessed May 01, 2018. https://www.youtube.com/watch?v=yWl77Tln5SE.

"Ron Popeil." Wikipedia. April 29, 2019. Accessed May 01, 2018. https://en.wikipedia.org/wiki/Ron_Popeil.

"Billy Mays." Wikipedia. April 22, 2019. Accessed May 01, 2018. https://en.wikipedia.org/wiki/Billy_Mays.

"About Shark Tank TV Show Series." ABC. Accessed May 01, 2018. https://abc.go.com/shows/shark-tank/about-the-show.

"About Shark Tank TV Show Series." ABC. Accessed May 01, 2018. https://abc.go.com/shows/shark-tank/about-the-show: 34, 42-55.

Field, Sarah, and Sarah Field. "The 'Shark Tank' Effect Can Fall Flat, As One Lori Greiner Investment Proved Two Years After Making a Deal." The Inquisitr. January 29, 2018. Accessed May 04, 2019. https://www.inquisitr.com/4759577/the-shark-tank-effect-can-fall-flat-as-one-lori-greiner-investment-proved-two-years-after-making-a-deal/.

"Thousands Per Minute." Cory Bergeron. Accessed May 04, 2019. http://corybergeron.com/.

Schneider, Joan, and Julie Hall. "Why Most Product Launches Fail." Harvard Business Review. August 01, 2014. Accessed May 01, 2018. https://hbr.org/2011/04/why-most-product-launches-fail.

Jordan, Scott. *Shark Bites: The Unofficial Guide to Shark Tank by Entrepreneurs from the Show*. Poodle Press, 2015.

"It is well settled that legal fees are not recoverable unless provided under the terms of a contract or authorized by statute." See, *U.S. Underwriters Ins. Co. v. City Club Hotel, LLC,* 3 N.Y.3d 592, 597, 789 N.Y.S.2d 470, 822 N.E.2d 777 [2004].

Resources, MPEP. "2701 Patent Term [R-07.2015]." 2701-Patent

Term. November 19, 2010. Accessed May 01, 2018. https://
www.uspto.gov/web/offices/pac/mpep/s2701.html.

Slater, Brian V., and John P. Dillon. "Preserving Provisional Rights
for Pre-Issuance Patent Damages." *Landslide - American Bar
Assoc.*10, No. 3 (January/February 2018). Accessed May 1, 2018.

"First Inventor to File (FITF) Resources." United States Patent
and Trademark Office - An Agency of the Department of
Commerce. Accessed May 01, 2018. https://www.uspto.gov/
patent/first-inventor-file-fitf-resources.

Wang, Lina. "The International Information and Library
Review." *Intellectual Property Protection in China,* Vol. 36, No. 3
(September 2004): 253-6.

Turnage, Mark. "A Mind-Blowing Number Of Counterfeit Goods
Come From China." Business Insider. June 25, 2013. Accessed
May 04, 2019. https://www.businessinsider.com/most-
counterfeit-goods-are-from-china-2013-6.

European Union Intellectual Property Office (EUIPO). EUIPO
and Europol. *2017 Situation Report on Counterfeiting and Piracy
in the European Union.* Spain, 2017. Accessed May 04, 2019.
Accessed May 01, 2018 https://www.europol.europa.eu/
publications-documents/2017-situation-report-counterfeiting-
and-piracy-in-european-union.

"How Long Does Copyright Protection Last?" Copyright.
Accessed May 04, 2019. https://www.copyright.gov/help/faq/
faq-duration.html.

"17 U.S. Code § 504 - Remedies for Infringement: Damages and
Profits." Legal Information Institute. Accessed May 01, 2018.
https://www.law.cornell.edu/uscode/text/17/504.

"Copyright Infringement -- First Sale Doctrine." The United States Department of Justice. September 19, 2018. Accessed May 01, 2018. https://www.justice.gov/jm/criminal-resource-manual-1854-copyright-infringement-first-sale-doctrine.

"Works Made for Hire." Library of Congress. Accessed May 01, 2018. https://www.copyright.gov/. Accessed May 01, 2018. https://www.copyright.gov/circs/circ09.pdf.

Kramer, Alexis. "Amazon Wins Knock-Off Pillow Fight." Bloomberg Law. May 23, 2017. Accessed May 01, 2018. https://www.bna.com/amazon-wins-knockoff-n73014451489/.

"Digital Millennium Copyright Act of 1998, 17 USC § 512." Legal Information Institute. Accessed May 04, 2019. https://www.law.cornell.edu/uscode/text/17/512.

Urquizu, Laura. "Counterfeiters to Target Millennial Shoppers on Black Friday." IPWatchdog.com | Patents & Patent Law. November 20, 2018. Accessed December 01, 2018. https://www.ipwatchdog.com/2018/11/20/counterfeiters-target-millennial-shoppers-black-friday/id=103419/.

Sutherland, Jessica. "What a Bunch of Turkeys!" Digital Law Group. November 20, 2018. Accessed May 04, 2019. http://www.digitallawgroup.com/what-a-bunch-of-turkeys/.

Ries, Al, Jack Trout, and Philip Kotler. *Positioning: The Battle for Your Mind*. New York, NY: McGraw-Hill Education, 2001.

Docie, Ronald Louis., and Ronald Louis. Docie. *The Inventors Bible: How to Market and License Your Brilliant Ideas*. Berkeley: Ten Speed Press, 2015.

Samson, Carl, and Benny Luo. "China Is Now Stealing Ideas Off Kickstarter and Launching Them Faster and Cheaper." October 18, 2016. Accessed May 04, 2019. https://nextshark.com/yekutiel-sherman-kickstarter-chinese-factory/.

"Registration Maintenance/Renewal/Correction Forms." United States Patent and Trademark Office - An Agency of the Department of Commerce. Accessed May 01, 2018. https://www.uspto.gov/trademarks-application-process/filing-online/registration-maintenancerenewalcorrection-forms.

Montgomery, Kate. "What Makes a Monster?: Monster Energy Company's History." Lawinspiring. March 08, 2018. Accessed November 01, 2018. https://lawinspiring.com/what-makes-a-monster/.

Phillips, Paula Brillson. "TO CATCH A THIEF...Intellectual Property Rights in Action." Brillson's Law. December 12, 2012. Accessed November 01, 2018. https://brillson.wordpress.com/2012/12/12/to-catch-a-thief-intellectual-property-rights-in-action/.

"RPX Market Sector Update: E-Commerce and Software." Rpxcorp.com. March 2018. Accessed May 04, 2019. http://www.rpxcorp.com/intelligence/patent-risk-digest/march-2018/.

Cushing, Tim. "It's Finally Over: 8 Years Of Mattel vs. Bratz And No One's Getting Paid But The Lawyers." Techdirt. January 29, 2013. Accessed May 04, 2019. https://www.techdirt.com/articles/20121019/17344420768/its-finally-over-8-years-mattel-vs-bratz-no-ones-getting-paid-lawyers.shtml.

Drummond, Mike. "Infomercial King - AJ Khubani." Inventors Digest. February 04, 2010. Accessed May 04, 2019. https://www.inventorsdigest.com/articles/infomercial-king-aj-khubani/.

Bieler, Peter, and Suzanne Costas. *This Business Has Legs: How L Used Infomercial Marketing to Create the $100,000,000, Thighmaster Exerciser.* New York, NY: J. Wiley, 1996.
Quinn, Gene, and Steve Brachmann. "US Inventor Sets Patents on Fire as Part of PTAB Protest at USPTO." IPWatchdog.com | Patents & Patent Law. August 13, 2017. Accessed May 04, 2019. https://www.ipwatchdog.com/2017/08/11/us-inventor-patents-on-fire-ptab-protest-uspto/id=86757/.

"Alice Corp. v. CLS Bank International." Wikipedia. December 07, 2018. Accessed May 04, 2019. https://en.wikipedia.org/wiki/Alice_Corp._v._CLS_Bank_International.

"US Inventor Rally." USI. August 11, 2017. Accessed May 01, 2018. https://www.usinventor.org/rally/.

Lynch, Jennifer. "Bunch O Balloons Patent Ruling Doubled to $24.5 Million." ANb Media, Inc. April 01, 2019. Accessed May 01, 2019. https://www.anbmedia.com/news/toys/2019/03/bunch-o-balloons-patent-ruling-doubled-to-24-5-million/.

Crum, Brooke. "Catfight: Lawsuit Alleges Springfield Company Used False Means to Sell Feline Toy." Leader. April 02, 2018. Accessed May 04, 2019. https://www.news-leader.com/story/news/local/ozarks/2018/04/02/catfight-lawsuit-alleges-springfield-company-used-false-means-sell-feline-toy/479392002/.

Kaplan, Michael. "Cat Fight! How These Inventors Beat the Counterfeiters That Nearly Destroyed Their Company." Entrepreneur. July 12, 2018. Accessed May 01, 2018. https://www.entrepreneur.com/article/315142.

INDEX